Questions and Answers

FRENCH

KEY STAGE 4

Steven Crossland

Principal Examiner

SERIES EDITOR: BOB McDUELL

Contents

HOW TO USE THIS BOOK

The aim of this book is to provide you, the student, with the help you need to reach the highest level of achievement possible at GCSE or, in Scotland, at General and Credit levels. The book is designed to help all students up to A* grade standard at GCSE.

Questions and Answers – French is designed to provide:

- Brief **revision summaries** and hints on the examination in general, identifying the important information you must understand if progress is to be made answering examination questions. Spend some time on these sections first and refer back to them whenever you find it necessary. There should not be anything in these sections which is brand new, but it is always useful to remind yourself of the important points about revision and examination procedure.

- **Advice** on each of the separate components or skill areas with hints on the different techniques required to perform to the highest standards. Notes are included about the nature of each different type of task that you are likely to encounter in the examination and guidance is given to enable you to gain practice at each stage.

- Many examples of **examination questions**. You will find that you will make progress by studying a wide range of questions and by heeding the guidance given on ways to improve or learn from answers given to these questions. The questions are either samples published by the various GCSE Examination Boards or newly prepared material of the type you are likely to meet in the examination.

- **Sample answers** to questions on the Speaking and Writing components. Although not always perfect answers, they point the way forward for you and perhaps they challenge you to do better. You can try the questions for yourself before checking the sample answers and you can then go on to try the other examples given. Answers to the Listening and Reading exercises are also given at the back of the book.

- **Examiner's tips and commentaries**. By using the experience of an Examiner you can gain advice which can enable you to see how your answers can be improved and hence ensure success.

- The **CD** which comes with the book contains material for the Speaking and Listening components. Details of this are given in the relevant sections of the book. The section on Speaking gives the teacher's part for the role plays and a large number of questions in French for you to practise, followed by sample answers, whilst the remainder of the CD contains the recorded material for the Listening exercises. The CD track points are indicated by a CD icon with the appropriate number inset.

GCSE FRENCH – WHAT DO I HAVE TO KNOW?

Whichever GCSE French examination you take, the same basic language skills are tested. These skills are:

- Speaking – the ability to make yourself understood when speaking French.
- Listening – the ability to understand spoken French.
- Reading – the ability to understand written French.
- Writing – the ability to make yourself understood in written French.

You don't have to be equally good at all these skills to be a good linguist, but normally competence in one skill area helps to give competence in the others. At GCSE all four of these skills are tested to an equal degree – they have 'equal weighting' – and they are tested at two levels which are referred to as the Foundation and the Higher tiers. Your teacher may decide that you will do some coursework (usually in Writing) instead of a final examination, but no more than 25% of the total marks can be assigned to coursework. You are likely to do your Speaking exam (the oral) before the written papers. For all four components or skill areas, you can choose the level to attempt (either Foundation or Higher Tier), but only by succeeding at the higher levels can you be assured of obtaining a top grade.

It is important to remember that you are not expected to be able to speak and write faultless French in order to get a good GCSE grade. After all, how many people speak and write their own language without error? None! The important thing, in speaking and writing any language, is to be understood or to communicate with reasonable clarity.

As for understanding written and spoken French (i.e. reading and listening comprehension), once again it is not necessary to be perfect – you are not expected to understand every single word. A very important skill in language is 'gist' comprehension – i.e. understanding the general idea of a passage of written or spoken French by being able to pick out certain words or phrases. There are pitfalls here, however – it is easy to misunderstand a sentence because, even though you are familiar with a number of words in it, you miss a key word such as a negative or the particular tense of a verb. At the Higher Tier, 'gist' understanding is tested to a greater depth and greater accuracy is expected in writing and speaking.

TOPICS AND SETTINGS

It is useful if you can obtain a copy of the syllabus or the 'Defined Content' for the examination for which you will be entered. As well as giving an outline of the topics you need to be familiar with, the Defined Content lists all the grammar structures that you are expected to know and also provides lists of the words that are required at Foundation level.

These lists of words vary slightly from one Board to another, but the topics tend to be the same for each. Check that you have learned the vocabulary and are able to write and speak about the following topic areas:

- **Personal identification**
- **Family, friends and social interaction**
- **House and home**
- **Daily routine**
- **Geographical surroundings – town and country**
- **School**
- **Work, careers, employment, future plans**
- **Hobbies, free time, sport and entertainments**
- **Travel, public and private transport**

- **Shopping**
- **Food and drink**
- **Holidays**
- **Accommodation** (hotels, campsites, youth hostels etc.)
- **Weather**
- **Health and welfare** (illness, emergencies, the chemists)
- **Work, education and future plans**
- **Services** (bank, post office, tourist office, lost property office, the police)

Sometimes you will have items in the examination that do not appear to fit neatly into any of the above topic areas, but they will normally be associated with one or more of these.

To find out what types of exercises you are likely to come across in the examination – read on! Within each section there is a range of exercises of the type that you may encounter in the exam. At the start of each section you will find the simpler Foundation Tier exercises. These lead on to the more demanding exercises that are set at the Higher Tier.

REVISION CHECKLIST

In order to help with your revision for the examination, you may find it useful to check that you have covered the points below. Do remember that this is only a very general checklist; you also need to refer to more detailed grammar summaries such as you will find in the back of your school textbook or in the *Letts GCSE French Study Guide*.

You should, however, make sure that you have covered the following thoroughly:

- **Key vocabulary** relating to the topics set out on page 2 above. For example: school subjects, forms of transport, holiday activities, common drinks and snacks, weather, etc.

- **Numbers**: all of them! Remember to be familiar with the sound as well as the sight of them (i.e. they need to be recognised in listening as well as in reading). Learn in particular the numbers 12 to 16, 70–80 and 90–100. Be clear about the difference in sound between *deux*, *dix* and *douze*. Remember how the sound of numbers can change according to the word that follows – e.g. in *dix francs* the number sounds as 'dee' whereas in *dix ans* it sounds as 'deez'. Don't forget to learn basic 'ordinal' numbers (*premier*, *deuxième*, etc.).

- **Times.**

- **Days, months, dates.**

- **Seasons** (e.g. *été*) and **festivals** (e.g. *Pâques*).

- **Directions** (*à gauche*, etc.) and **positions** (*près de*, *à côté de*, *devant*, etc.).

- **Countries** and **nationalities** (e.g. *Allemagne*, *allemand*).

- **Question words**: *qui*; *quel/quelle/quels/quelles*; *où*; *quand*; *combien*; *comment*; *pourquoi*; *qu'est-ce que*; *est-ce que*; *lequel/laquelle*, etc.

- **Descriptions** of people and things; learn the rules of adjective agreement (*les yeux bleus*; *une petite voiture*).

- **Phrases to describe feelings, opinions and emotions** (e.g. *j'étais déçu(e)*; *c'était ennuyeux*; *je pense que c'est formidable*; *j'ai peur*, etc.).

Verbs

You must be familiar with the use of verbs in the following tenses:

(Note: examples given below are all in the first person singular (i.e. *je*) forms. You should also be able to use the other forms, in particular *il/elle/on*, *nous* and *ils/elles*.)

Present: *je mange*; *je vais*; *je me lève*; *je n'aime pas*.

Perfect: *j'ai joué*; *j'ai vu*; *je suis allé(e)*; *je suis parti(e)*; *je me suis reposé(e)*; *je n'ai pas décidé*.

Future: either *je vais passer*; *je ne vais pas travailler*, *je vais me coucher*.

or *je passerai*; *je ne travaillerai pas*; *je ne me coucherai pas*.

Imperfect: *je faisais*; *j'habitais*; *j'étais*; *j'allais*; *je n'avais pas*; *je me détendais*.

(Note: use *il faisait* to say what the weather was like; otherwise use *c'était for* 'it was' and *il y avait* for 'there was/were'.)

You will also have used the **conditional** tense (e.g. 'I would buy'). Use the future stem and add the imperfect ending (*j'achèterais*).

It is also quite easy, and good style, to use the **pluperfect** tense (e.g. 'I had lost'). Form this as for the perfect tense but use the imperfect tense forms of *avoir* (or *être*) – e.g. *j'avais perdu*, *j'étais retournée*.

Learn the following irregular **perfect tense** forms:

AVOIR – *j'ai eu* (I have had)	BOIRE – *j'ai bu* (I drank)
COURIR – *j'ai couru* (I ran)	DEVOIR – *j'ai dû* (I had to)
DIRE – *j'ai dit* (I said/told)	ÉCRIRE – *j'ai écrit* (I wrote)
ÊTRE – *j'ai été* (I have been)	FAIRE – *j'ai fait* (I did/made)
LIRE – *j'ai lu* (I have read)	METTRE – *j'ai mis* (I have put)
NAÎTRE – *je suis né(e)* (I was born)	OUVRIR – *j'ai ouvert* (I opened)
PLEUVOIR – *il a plu* (it rained)	POUVOIR – *j'ai pu* (I have been able)
PRENDRE – *j'ai pris* (I took)	RECEVOIR – *j'ai reçu* (I received)
(SOU)RIRE – *j'ai (sou)ri* (I smiled/laughed)	VENIR – *je suis venu(e)* (I came)
VOIR – *j'ai vu* (I saw)	

Learn the list of verbs that use *être* in the perfect (and pluperfect):

ALLER	ARRIVER	DESCENDRE	ENTRER	MONTER
MOURIR	NAÎTRE	PARTIR	RENTRER	RESTER
RETOURNER	SORTIR	TOMBER	VENIR (DEVENIR, REVENIR)	

Learn the **imperfect/conditional** tense endings:

je/tu ...ais; *il/elle/on ...ait*; *nous ...ions*; *vous ...iez* ; *ils/elles ...aient*

(The above endings are added to the stem of the verb for the imperfect tense and to the infinitive (in most cases) for the conditional.)

Learn the **future** tense endings:

je ...ai; *tu ....as*; *il/elle/on ...a*; *nous ...ons*; *vous ...ez*; *ils/elles ...ont*

Generally these endings are added to the infinitive, e.g.

je parlerai (I will speak)

elle finira (she will finish)

but there are a number of common irregular verbs in the future which you need to learn separately, e.g.

ÊTRE – *je serai* (I will be) AVOIR – *j'aurai* (I will have)
FAIRE – *je ferai* (I will make/do) ALLER – *j'irai* (I will go)
DEVOIR – *je devrai* (I will have to) ENVOYER – *j'enverrai* (I will send)
POUVOIR – *je pourrai* (I will be able to) RECEVOIR – *je recevrai* (I will receive)
VENIR – *je viendrai* (I will come) VOIR – *je verrai* (I will see)
VOULOIR – *je voudrai* (I will want).

Note also:

il faudra (it will be necessary)   *il pleuvra* (it will rain).

PARTICULAR FEATURES OF THE EXAMINATION

- French/English dictionaries can be used for most of the exam.
- Most of the questions on the Reading and Listening papers are in French. Where the questions are given in French, answers are to be written in French.
- There is much use of 'visuals', particularly at the Foundation Tier.
- Many exercises require box-ticking, matching, form-filling, etc.
- On most papers, instructions or 'rubrics' are given in French.

Here are some further points about the above

Dictionaries: you can choose which dictionary to use. You should have one which you take to each French lesson. The one you are used to should be the one you take into the exam as you know your way around it. You are not allowed to use electronic dictionaries or translating machines in the exam. The dictionary you choose to use should be of the 'bilingual' type, with one half giving French words with their English meanings and the other half listing English words with French equivalents. You must be familiar with your dictionary and gain as much practice as you can in using it. Practice will also teach you about the pitfalls involved in using a dictionary.

For most Examination Boards you will be able to refer to your dictionary as you wish during the Reading and the Writing exam. A dictionary will be available to you during your preparation time for the oral exam, but you will not be able to refer to it once you start the actual speaking test. The use of dictionaries is generally not allowed in Listening examinations as the turning of pages would be too much of a distraction to other candidates.

Although you will be able to refer to your dictionary whenever you like during the Reading and Writing exams, you must remember that these are timed tests – you will not have time to check each word and in any case there is no need to look up words which you already know. You will find a little more advice on using dictionaries later on in this book in the examination hints sections for the appropriate parts of the exam.

Questions in French: on the Reading and Listening papers, questions in French must be answered in French. However, you are not required to write full sentences and, as long as you show in your answer that you have understood the French in the text, you will not lose marks for errors of written French, as long as what you have written would be understood by a French person. If a question requires an answer using a number (a time or someone's age, for example), it is acceptable to write a number rather than the word. However, if it is a time, remember to avoid writing it in the English style such as '8 o'clock' or '8 pm' – write *8h.* or *8 heures.*

Use of visuals: you will need to be familiar with the style of pictures or drawings used in the exams. You can be quite sure that the Examination Boards will have done everything they can to make them clear and unambiguous and they should not cause you any problems. At the same time, study them carefully in the exam so that you can be quite sure of what they represent.

Box-ticking, form-filling, etc.: here again, you need to be clear about what you are required to do. In most cases, an example question and answer will be given at the start of an exercise, so be sure to study it carefully so that you know how to proceed. When ticking boxes, circling letters, etc., make sure that your intended answer is clear. If you change your mind, make it clear to the examiner what your final answer is. Never try to cheat by writing one answer on top of another or ticking two boxes when only one should be ticked – you will lose the mark automatically.

French instructions: You need to be familiar with the meanings of French rubrics or instructions. As mentioned above, an example question and answer at the start of an exercise will often tell you what you have to do, but it is important that, in the year leading up to the exam, you become familiar with the meanings of the French instructions. You will have seen examples in your textbook and your teacher will have told you about them, but here is a checklist of some common ones:

Répondez en français – Answer in French
Répondez en chiffres – Answer in figures
Cochez la bonne case (les bonnes cases) – Tick the appropriate box (boxes)
Lisez les questions – Read the questions
Regardez les dessins/images – Look at the drawings/pictures
Pour chaque question/personne... – For each question/person...
Remplissez les blancs – Fill in the blanks
Complétez la grille – Fill in the grid
Faites correspondre... – Match up...
Encerclez... – Draw a circle round...
Si la phrase/affirmation est vraie, cochez la case 'vrai' – If the sentence/statement is true, tick the 'true' box
Puis corrigez l'affirmation – Then correct the statement
Choisissez la description qui correspond le mieux – Choose the description which best fits
Vous n'aurez pas besoin de toutes les lettres – You will not need to use all the letters
Vous allez entendre une conversation/interview, etc. – You are going to hear a conversation/interview, etc.
Vous entendrez la conversation deux fois – You will hear the conversation twice
Écoutez encore une fois – Listen again
Donnez ou demandez les détails/les renseignements suivants – Give or ask for the following details/information
Préparez les questions suivantes – Prepare the following tasks
Écrivez une lettre de 100 à 150 mots – Write a letter of 100 to 150 words
Décrivez... – Describe...
Ce que vous avez fait/Ce que vous allez faire – What you have done/What you are going to do

REVISION HINTS

Confidence in speaking French is the key to success in the other skills and confidence comes from regular practice. You don't have to be in class to practise speaking French – you don't even have to be with anyone else! Decide to speak French to yourself on your way to school or on a Sunday afternoon, for instance. Agree to chat in French with a friend preparing for the exam with you.

The oral exam will always include a **general conversation** section in which you are asked questions about everyday topics such as: yourself and your family, your home, your town and village, your interests or pastimes, your school and your holidays. You may also be asked about things that you have done (how you spent the weekend, the last holidays, any visits to France) – where obviously your skill in using the past tense is being tested – or what you plan to do next weekend, during the next holidays, after the exams or as a career, to test your ability to use the future tense. These, then, are the topics that you should practise talking about.

You will also have to perform **role plays** in French. In order to practise for this, imagine yourself in those situations which you have worked on during your French studies – in a shop, a café, a restaurant, a station, a tourist office etc. And remember to practise talking about awkward situations or complaining – the car has broken down, the chips are cold, you've lost your wallet, etc.

You may have had to prepare a short talk for the examination. It goes without saying that you need to practise this regularly so that you can deliver it with confidence in the exam. Try recording yourself giving your talk before the exam. Play it back and consider how you might improve on it. In the exam, however, be prepared to answer questions on your talk and try not to recite it too mechanically, otherwise it will sound as if you have simply learned it word-for-word.

In the Speaking section on the CD you will hear examples of different parts of the oral exam with 'model' answers. You will hear some role plays with 'beeps' for you to stop and supply the missing details, based on the instructions given. Then, you will hear a large number of general questions for which you can practise giving the answers. Don't forget that no oral examination is like another – you will certainly be asked some of the questions on the recording but it is up to your teacher, working from the examination instructions, to decide which questions to ask you.

EXAMINATION HINTS

Speak French to yourself on the day of the examination as soon as you get up. Report for the examination on time. Avoid having to rush at all costs. You will probably feel nervous but you must remember that your teacher wants you to do well and may be nervous as well! Use your preparation time wisely – talk through your part of the role plays quietly and make judicious use of the dictionary (see below). Don't worry if you make some mistakes – everybody does. Don't be afraid to restart a sentence if you get into difficulties but remember that you can be given no credit for any answers given in English!

Using the dictionary

A dictionary will be available during your preparation time but you will not be able to take it with you into the examination room. Although you may be able to make notes, you will not have time to write down all the words that you have looked up in the dictionary and in any case you must remember that it is not isolated words but coherent phrases that you must utter in the role plays. Use the dictionary to look for words that you have genuinely forgotten or do not know but do not aim to spend too much of the preparation time searching through it. You are not likely to be able to remember all of the words and it is more important to have a practice run through the role play rather than spending all your time with your nose in the dictionary.

You will have realised during your rehearsal for the oral examination that there are certain words that you do not need to look up. Take the following English instruction by way of example (you will find that the instructions for the role plays are usually given in English):

'Ask if there are any rooms available.'

There is obviously no need to look up the French for 'available'. You use an expression that you will have learned such as:

Vous avez des chambres de libre?

The same would apply to an instruction such as:

'Find out if it is possible to travel that morning.'

No need to use the dictionary here, as you have learned the expression:

Est-ce qu'il y a des départs ce matin?

You may need to use the French to English part of the dictionary. In the Higher Tier role plays, cues are often given in the form of short French phrases (though often accompanied by a small picture to clarify the meaning) and you may wish to check up on the meaning.

It is important, then, not to overuse the dictionary during your preparation time. This time passes quickly and the more you look up in the dictionary the more nervous you are likely to become. It is better to practise the role plays quietly to yourself, looking up the occasional word which you may have forgotten and which is vital for communicating the message.

Visuals

Cues for the role plays are often given in the form of pictures and/or symbols. You will have practised using these in class and you will see a number of examples in the following pages. The meaning of the pictures should be quite clear but you must not worry if there is more than one possible interpretation of the picture; the examiner will have been instructed to accept any sensible interpretation. For example:

For this cue you could say:

Il y a des trains pour Paris? or:

Le train pour Paris est parti? or:

Est-ce que ce train va à Paris? or:

Le train s'arrête à Paris? or several others.

With the visuals, then, simply be sure that you convey what you assume to be the required message. If it is really not clear you should say to your teacher:

Je suis désolé(e) Monsieur/Madame – je ne comprends pas ce dessin.

but it is unlikely that you will need to resort to this!

REVISION SUMMARY

If you need to revise this subject more thoroughly, see the relevant topics in the *Letts* GCSE *French Study Guide*.

ROLE PLAYS

In a role play you follow instructions as if you were in a particular situation in a French-speaking country.

Usually the situation involves some sort of 'transaction' – i.e. you are buying something in a shop or café or booking in at a hotel or asking for information at a station, tourist office, etc. Your teacher or examiner plays the part of the salesperson or assistant.

Sometimes you have to imagine that you are in a situation with a pen-friend or exchange partner and are discussing something such as where to go or what to do. In this case, your teacher plays the part of the French pen-friend or partner.

Tu or *vous*?

It is important to remember that, in the 'transactional' type of role play, where you are talking with someone whom you don't really know, you MUST use *vous* when addressing that person. This is the formal word used in French for 'you' when talking with a stranger. In the second type of role play when you are addressing a pen-friend or partner, it is obviously more appropriate to use the *tu* or informal word for 'you'. This is probably the form you will use with your teacher in the conversation section of the oral.

Right or wrong?

Remember that the object is to convey the message on each task. Your teacher/examiner will give you credit as long as he or she thinks that a French person would understand what you mean. Bear in mind the point made in the general oral hints that the picture cues can sometimes be interpreted in various ways

FOUNDATION

Here are some Foundation level role plays in which the information you must give is provided in picture form. Note that the instructions are written in English (this will normally be the case in the speaking tasks). Remember that you have a few minutes to prepare them before you start. You shouldn't need to use the dictionary for these, but you may do so to check the occasional word if you wish. Remember, however, that finding the word in the dictionary doesn't tell you how to pronounce it (unless you are familiar with the phonetic alphabet used in dictionaries) – there is no point in using a word in French if you pronounce it incorrectly! That is why in most cases using the dictionary will serve as confirmation of a word that you have already learned: when seeing it in print, you will recall how it is pronounced.

> When you are ready, listen to the speaking section on the CD. When you hear a tone, stop your machine and give the appropriate response. Then play on to hear the suggested answer. If you made any mistakes, have another go later.
>
> Don't forget that the recorded versions are only examples and that there are usually several correct ways of carrying out the tasks.

TASK A

You are shopping in a grocer's in France.

Your teacher will play the part of the grocer and will start the conversation.

 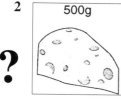 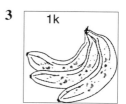 

MEG specimen

The question mark written to the right of a box indicates that this is something which you must ask for (in this case asking for some cheese/if they sell cheese and, in the final sub-task, asking how much you have to pay). In the case of points 2, 3 and 4 you make statements about what you would like (and how much). It wouldn't matter, however, if you put any of these in the form of a question, such as:
Est-ce que je peux avoir un kilo de bananes?
It's generally best, however, to convey the message in the simplest form:
(Je voudrais) un kilo de bananes.
Don't worry about losing marks for missing a detail at your first attempt – it will be up to your teacher to make the necessary prompt:
You: *Je voudrais des bananes.*
Teacher: *Vous en voulez combien?*
You: *Un kilo s'il vous plaît.*

You have arrived at a French hotel. You would like rooms for your family.

TASK B

Your teacher will play the part of the receptionist and will start the conversation.

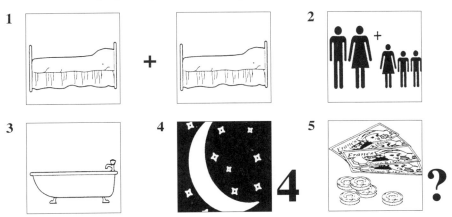

MEG specimen

Note how, as in the previous role play, you are told that your teacher will start the conversation. There will be no surprises here – he/she will simply open with something like: *Qu'y a-t-il pour votre service?* or *Je peux vous aider?* or just *Bonsoir!*
Furthermore, your teacher will ask questions or make comments after each of your responses. Remember that the situation is a transaction in which both of you are involved – so listen to what your teacher says.

In this next example symbols as well as pictures are used.

TASK C

You are at the café and need to buy two items from those given on the next page. Remember to greet the waiter and end the conversation politely.

ULEAC specimen

TASK D

Role plays can sometimes be set in the context of a stay with your penfriend. Here, there are verbal instructions as well as pictures – *répondez* ('answer') and *expliquez* ('explain').

You are staying with your pen-friend and you don't feel well.

Your teacher will play the part of your pen-friend and will start the conversation.

A: Répondez: **B: Expliquez:**

A: Répondez: **B: Expliquez ce que vous allez faire:**

NEAB specimen

At this level, pictures are not as likely to be used. The opening setting will generally be given in English, but the instructions will be given in French. The role plays are more 'open' than at Foundation Tier – that is to say, you can make up certain details rather than being told exactly what to say.

They will be more demanding than at Foundation Tier in various ways:

- tasks are more complex and will often include more than one element;
- they will be longer than at Foundation Tier;
- the vocabulary required will be more complex;
- you are likely to need tenses other than just the present;
- some tasks could well be 'unprepared' – that is, you will not know what is required until your teacher asks the question; the instruction on your card will simply be something like: *Répondez à la question de l'employé*;
- you may be required to express an appropriate emotion such as disappointment or anger.

Take time and care preparing role plays at this level. Use your dictionary, if necessary, to check on any words in the instructions that you do not understand, but don't forget that a particular part of a verb (e.g. *pourrez*) will not be there. Remember the advice given earlier not to spend all your time looking up words – it is better to practise your part during the preparation time. Try to predict what the unprepared question might be. Work out the simplest way of expressing the ideas in each task. Usually there will be more than one mark per sub-task available, so you can gain credit for partially correct responses, though as in all role plays, marks are awarded on the basis of how well you would be understood by a French person.

En panne

You are in France with your family. Your car has broken down on Route Nationale 28 (N28) near Rouen. You telephone a garage.
Your teacher will play the part of the garage owner and will start the conversation.

1 Donnez votre nom et dites pourquoi vous téléphonez.

2 Dites où vous êtes.

3 Donnez la marque et la couleur de la voiture.

4 Expliquez votre problème (freins? moteur? pneus? démarrage?)

5 Répondez à la question du garagiste. Remerciez le garagiste.

MEG specimen

Examiner's tip Notice how the key phrase *en panne* is given as a title. You could look for it in the dictionary of course, but it saves a bit of time! Be on the look out for the 'double questions' (1, 3 and 5 all require two pieces of information).

This next example concerns lost property – another commonly used topic in role plays. Notice again the unprepared and the double questions.

You have arrived in France on holiday and have lost your suitcase at the station. You go to the station lost property office and talk to the employee (played by your teacher).

1 Expliquez la situation.

2 Décrivez votre valise (donnez DEUX détails).

3 Dites où vous avez perdu votre valise.

4 Répondez à la question de l'employé.

5 Dites où on peut vous contacter en France.

> **Examiner's tip** In reporting an item of lost property, remember that you will be using past tenses – the perfect to report the loss (*j'ai perdu...*) and the imperfect to say what you were doing or where you were (*je faisais des courses*; *j'étais à la gare*) and also to describe the item and say what was in it (using *c'était...* and *il y avait...*). For the final line, however, the past tense would obviously be inappropriate. Note the use of *il y a* for 'ago'

TASK G

Now try this example in which you are being interviewed for a job.

You have applied to work in a French hotel and have been called for interview. Your teacher will play the part of the hotel owner who will interview you for the job.

1 Donnez votre nom et votre nationalité.

2 Dites pourquoi vous êtes venu(e) à l'hôtel.

3 Dites quelle expérience vous avez du travail. Donnez deux détails.

4 Dites quelle sorte de travail vous voudriez faire à l'hôtel.

5 Dites quand vous pourrez commencer à travailler à l'hôtel.

> **Examiner's tip** Interview situations are likely material for role plays. Be prepared for this by being able to spell your name, give your nationality and your experience of work. Note how important it is to be familiar with the different French question words such as *Quand?* (line 5) – 'when'? Remember that, in giving details of work's experience (line 3), you must use the past tense. *Pourrez* (line 5) is the future tense of *pouvoir* (meaning 'will be able'); although this is irregular, remember that in using it in the *je* form *(pourrai)*, it will sound exactly the same as it does in the *vous* form which you will hear when the question is asked.

Here is an example to practise in which you imagine that you are unwell and are seeing a doctor.

While on holiday in France you feel unwell with a bad stomach ache so you go to see the doctor.

Your teacher will play the part of the doctor and will start the conversation.

1   Dites au médecin où vous avez mal.

2   Répondez à la question du médecin.

3   Dites au médecin ce que vous avez mangé et bu.

4   Dites quand vous allez rentrer en Angleterre.

5   Demandez où se trouve la pharmacie.

> **Examiner's tip**   Again (line 1) note the need to know question words well – and remember to read the English introduction as it gives you the answer to the doctor's first question. Be aware of the need to use different tenses – the present in line 1, the perfect in line 3 and the future (with *aller*) in line 4. Note also that, since line 5 is written in French, it makes it very easy to ask the question! It won't always be as easy as this, but take advantage of any clues of this sort.

Here is a final role play situation of this style, using the road accident topic. This is a commonly set topic and you should learn the appropriate vocabulary.

While in France you witness an accident between a car and a cyclist and the police ask you some questions about it.

Your teacher will play the part of the police officer and will start the conversation.

1   Donnez votre nom et votre adresse en France.

2   Dites à quelle heure l'accident s'est passé.

3   Décrivez la voiture.

4   Décrivez le cycliste.

5   Répondez à la question de l'agent de police.

> **Examiner's tip**   Note how these role plays are gradually becoming more 'open' – that is, you are left to make up details yourself. Make sure you know the vital word *décrivez* (describe), though remember that the examiner is just as likely to use the question word *comment ... ?* In giving an address in France (line 1) try to make up a realistic one by using *l'auberge de jeunesse à Calais* (this would be quite sufficient) or, if you prefer to give an actual address, something like *vingt, rue de la Gare*. Notice again how important it is to be able to use different tenses.

HIGHER

The most demanding speaking exercises set at Higher Tier expect a good command of different tenses and require you to take the initiative. You may have to give an account in the past tense of an accident that you have witnessed or a journey that you have made. You may have to imagine that you are in a job interview situation. You may be asked to take part in a fairly long discussion about a particular topic.

At this level you need to be able to improvise; you are not given separate tasks to perform as much as a situation which you must describe. You will be assessed on the accuracy and fluency of your French, your accent, your command of verbs in different tenses and the range of vocabulary used – in short, the standard of your French and the ability you display in making yourself understood in a particular situation. You also need to show that you can understand and answer any questions put by your teacher. Be careful not to miss out any details mentioned in the instructions, or you could lose marks.

Here are two examples for you to practise.

TASK J

The notes and pictures below give an outline of an accident during a skiing holiday in Switzerland.

Tell the Examiner what happened. You need not mention every detail but you must cover the whole day's events,

Be prepared to respond to any questions or comments from the Examiner.

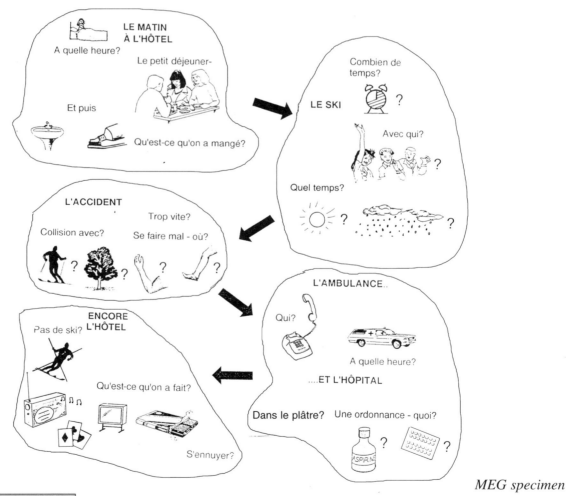

MEG specimen

Examiner's tip Some verb prompts are given in the infinitive (e.g. *se faire mal, s'ennuyer*) but you obviously have to put them into the correct form. It is clear from the question *Qu'est-ce qu'on a fait?* that the past tenses must be used. Be sure to learn the past tense forms of reflexive verbs (learn *je me suis levé/e* and base any others on this).

TASK K

Here finally is an example of a job interview situation. It is more complex than the interview in Task G because it will last longer and you do not know in advance exactly what questions you will be asked.

You see this advertisement for summer jobs at Euro Disney and decide to ring up to give details about yourself and to find out more information. The Examiner will begin the conversation.

10000 OFFRES D'EMPLOI

SAISON ÉTÉ 1998

vendeurs/vendeuses

serveurs/serveuses

Euro Disney

Tél. 00 33 7539 45

■ **Raison pour ton appel**

■ **Détails personnels**

■ **Heures de travail?**

ULEAC specimen

Examiner's tip Obviously the nature of this situation means that some of it will be 'unprepared', but during your preparation time think of likely questions that you might be asked in an interview such as experience of work, the dates you are available etc. Note that you will in places need the conditional tense to say 'I would like to work...' or 'I would be able to start...'. Remember that these verbs must be followed by an infinitive. Be sure to learn *je voudrais* or *j'aimerais* ('I would like') and *je pourrais* ('I would be able').

GENERAL CONVERSATION

Now you will hear on the disk some questions (about 100 in fact!) to practise for the General Conversation section of your oral exam. Whatever exam syllabus you are preparing for, you will be required to answer questions of this type. Concentrate on giving brief, precise answers to the questions. However, you should always aim to answer in a full sentence and be as accurate as you can. Obviously you will sometimes use English if giving the name of your favourite TV programme or pop star, but you must include French in your answer by saying, for example: *Mon chanteur préféré, c'est...*

There is a 'bleep' after each question for you to pause the machine and give your answer. You then play on and listen to the sample answer.

Practise the questions on a regular basis, taking one of the following eight topics in each session. Listen carefully to the model answers and see if your answers follow the same pattern.

[13] • Personal identity – self and family
[14] • House, home, geographical surroundings
[15] • Daily routine at home
[16] • Interests and pastimes
[17] • School
[18] • Past events
[19] • Holidays
[20] • Future plans

EXTENDED CONVERSATION

Now you can practise talking on the following topics at length rather than simply answering each separate question individually – the 'extended conversation' often used at the Higher Tier.

The three topics with an asterisk have been recorded as sample conversations.

[21] *Parle-moi de ta famille.**
Parle-moi de ta maison.
Parle-moi un peu de ce qui t'intéresse.
Parle-moi de ton école.
Raconte-moi une journée typique.
Dis-moi ce que tu fais d'habitude le weekend.
Parle-moi un peu de ta ville ou de ton village.

[22] *Dis-moi ce que tu as fait le weekend dernier.**

[23] *Parle-moi de ce que tu feras plus tard.**
Parle-moi de ce que tu aimerais faire comme métier.

In the three sample conversations, you will hear a general question on the topic to get you started. Once you hear the 'starter question', stop the CD and try to talk for a minute or two about the subject. Then play on, and answer the questions put by the 'teacher' on the recording. Note how the speaker giving the sample answers deals with the examiner's questions. Note too how the speakers are not 'word perfect' – they sometimes hesitate a little or restart a sentence. It is therefore perfectly all right for you to do the same! But try to fill in your pauses with French words or 'grunts' – don't say 'um', say *euh*... Listen to how the French speaker fills in the pauses, and try to practise including appropriate fill-in words and phrases, which, although they mean very little, sound very French! Again, practise this on a regular basis, including the other topics which are not on the recording.

In the exam, too, your teacher will make a conversation about the subject by asking questions during your talk. The idea is not that you should recite a learnt speech, but that you should be able to link up sentences and answer any questions your teacher might include.

Here are some useful fill-in words and phrases: *alors, eh bien, ben, tu vois, tu comprends, enfin, euh, c'est-à-dire.*

REVISION HINTS

You need as much practice as you can get in listening to French. Obviously you will have the chance to practise in class by listening to your teacher and to recordings. But you should try to listen to French at other times: French radio, French films on British television, etc.

Don't get depressed when you discover that you can't understand much of the French that is being said. They do seem to speak very fast! But it's useful to try to pick out words or get the general gist of what is being said. And remember that the more practice you get in listening, the more your comprehension skills will improve.

Finally, try to arrange from time to time to speak French with your friends who are also preparing for the exam. By talking French with others you will be gaining extra practice in listening as well as in speaking. If by any chance you have a French pen-friend or exchange partner, ask him or her to send you a taped message in French or to make some recordings from French radio or TV for you. And of course, if you are lucky enough to be able to visit France, whether on a trip or exchange, make the most of it: you will have a marvellous opportunity to listen to French being spoken in all sorts of situations.

EXAMINATION HINTS

On the day of the listening exam, practise talking French to yourself or your friends as you go to the exam. There is not a lot of point in reading through sheets of vocabulary lists at this stage, but 'tuning in' to the language on the day of the exam will be helpful.

Read all questions and instructions carefully. You will have been told this many times by your teacher and the notes on the examination paper will remind you about it, but it is vitally important. As you read the questions, be alert to exactly what is being asked for. Don't read too quickly. It's surprising how easy it is, particularly when under exam stress, to read a *quand...?* as a *qui...?*. It is sometimes useful, when reading the questions, to underline the key words in order to avoid errors (e.g. *donnez <u>deux</u> raisons*; *qu'est-ce qu'il <u>n'aime pas</u> faire?*).

Make use of the time given for reading and answering the questions. Never rush. Even for what appear to be easy questions, use the time given for reading and answering wisely. You would be very annoyed if you found out later that you had missed part of an answer by rushing.

Listen to all playings. You will normally hear the French texts two or three times. Don't ignore the later playings. Very often something which is not clear on the first listening will become clearer when you hear it again. Even if you are confident that you have the answer from the first playing, listen anyway to subsequent playings – you may discover that you have misheard it. In any case you will use any later playings to check your answers carefully.

Make sure you can hear the recording. If you cannot hear the tape as clearly as you should be able to, it is most important that you let the invigilator know at the very start of the exam (during the introductory comments, for instance). You must not allow yourself to be put off, for example, by the continuous noise of a lawn-mower outside. It is up to you to let the invigilator know if there is anything that might be affecting your ability to hear the tape as clearly as possible.

Answer the questions fully – and legibly. This applies equally to the Reading paper. When you have written your answer, check that it is a full answer to the question (though never write more than is required by the question). Is your answer clear? Have you shown that you have understood the French? As far as you can be sure, would a French person understand what your answer means? Will the examiner know what you mean and be able to read what you have written? Have you answered in the correct language (sometimes you will be required to answer in English)? If you have changed your answer, will the examiner know which one to mark?

If you need to revise this subject more thoroughly, see the relevant topics in the *Letts* GCSE French Study Guide.

LISTENING QUESTIONS

On the Foundation Tier Listening exercises, you are generally asked to pick out individual items such as numbers, days, times, prices, details of people's likes and so on and to write them down in French (sometimes in English) or in figures. Sometimes you have to match up written statements or pictures with what you hear or take your pick from alternatives by ticking the appropriate box (remember the instruction *Cochez la bonne case* or *Cochez la case appropriée*).

The detail you are listening out for will usually be quite clear and will often be followed by a pause on the tape for you to write or tick the answer. You sometimes have to listen to a little more and perhaps then write more than one answer but, although you must not waste time, you should not find that you will be too rushed to write down your answers.

Usually at the start of the test there will be a few short items in which you have to listen out for a particular detail (the question will make it quite clear what you are listening for). The French here is often in the form of announcements or instructions.

Here are a few examples. You should be at the start of the Listening section on the CD.

Note that in order to give plenty of examples on the recording, each French sentence or text in these exercises is played ONCE only and there are no built-in pauses for writing answers: you have to pause the machine yourself. (In the examination, you will usually hear the French stimulus twice.) When you hear the 'bleep', replay the sentence or exercise in order to hear it for a second time. However, to give you an idea of what the exam is like, listen to each stimulus no more than twice.

TASK A

It is quite possible that you will start off with a few simple examples where English is used. A small amount of the Listening and the Reading papers do use English, often at the start of the paper. You are usually required to tick boxes.

Here, then, are a few examples of such questions.

1 When you arrive in Lannion, you go straight to a hotel and ask if they have any rooms. The manager tells you how much the rooms cost per night.

How much is each room?

A 50 Francs   **B** 150 Francs   **C** 200 Francs   **D** 250 Francs   (1)

2 You ask for some details of the rooms offered.

What type of room are you offered?   (1)

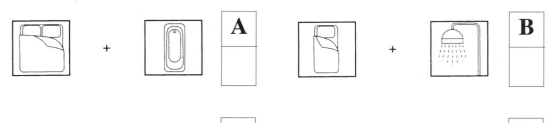

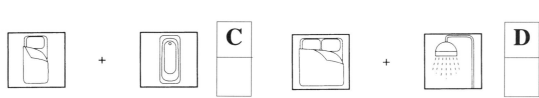

3   You are both hungry so you ask the manager when they start serving the evening meal.

When does the manager say they start to serve it?   (1)

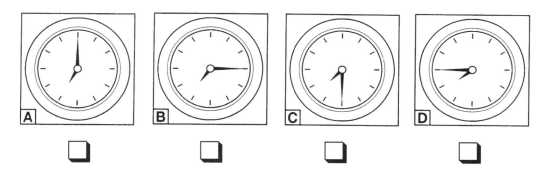

4   You want to go to the town centre, so you ask someone at the hotel how to get there.

How does she suggest getting there?   (1)

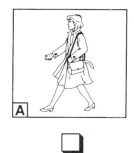
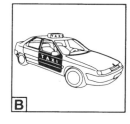
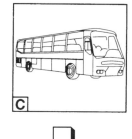
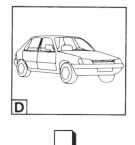

5   Later on, in town, you ask a couple how to get to the cinema. They tell you the way.

Where is the cinema?   (1)

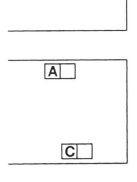
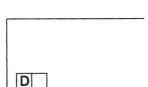
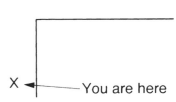

MEG specimen

As already pointed out, the instructions to the Listening exercises are usually in French. In the early exercises, however, the instructions are brief, they will use French phrases that you will have learned and they will normally include an example.

Here is a fairly simple example using orders for drinks and snacks in a café.

Au Café

Qu'est-ce qu'ils prennent?

Choisis la bonne image. Écris la lettre dans la case.

Boissons

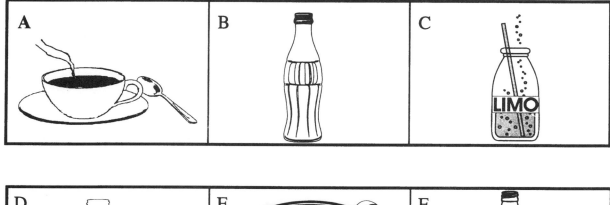

Exemple: **E**

1 ☐　　　2 ☐　　　3 ☐　　　4 ☐

(4)

Snacks

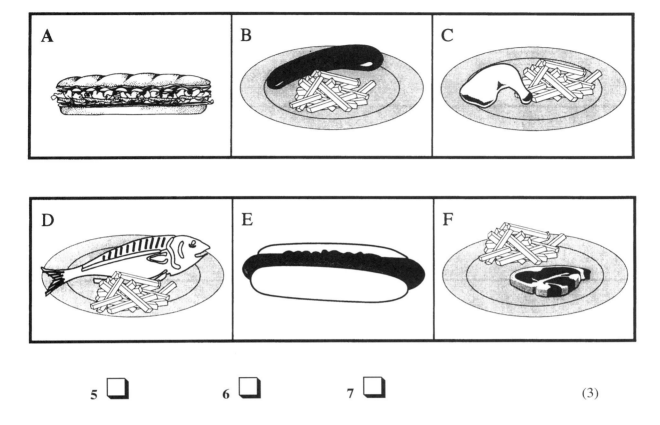

5 ☐   6 ☐   7 ☐   (3)

ULEAC specimen

In these next few examples, you again simply tick boxes, though there are a couple of variations, one where you write an arrow and another where you write in figures. However, all the instructions in these are given in French.

TASK C

TRACK 27

Un jour, le frère de Dominique est malade.

1 Où est-ce qu'il a mal?

Cochez la bonne case.

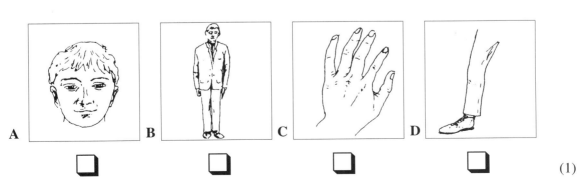

A   B   C   D

☐   ☐   ☐   ☐   (1)

David, un ami de Dominique, vient à la maison.

Il parle de sa famille.

2 Quelle image correspond à la description? **Cochez la bonne case.**

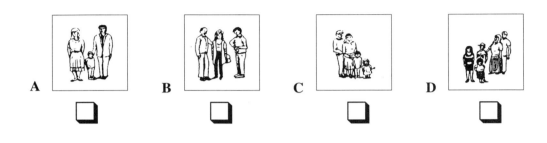

(1)

3 Où habite David? **Indiquez avec une flèche.** ⟵

4 ème
3 ème
2 ème
1 er
R de C

(1)

Dominique vous parle de ce que vous allez manger.

4 Qu'est-ce que c'est? **Cochez la bonne case.**

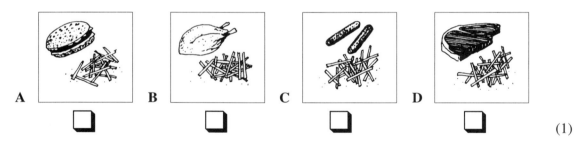

(1)

5 A quelle heure est-ce que vous allez manger? **Ecrivez l'heure** (en chiffres).

(1)

6 Qu'est-ce que vous allez faire cet après-midi? **Cochez la bonne case.**

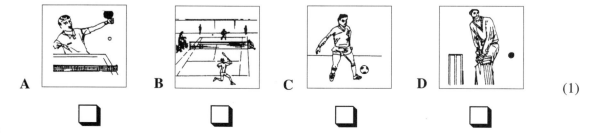

(1)

More box-ticking, but the French you read and hear is now becoming more complex.

1 Un soir, la mère de Jean-André sort des photos de famille. Elle vous montre une photo d'un groupe de jeunes enfants. Elle vous dit:

Quelle est l'image qui correspond à la description de Jean-André?

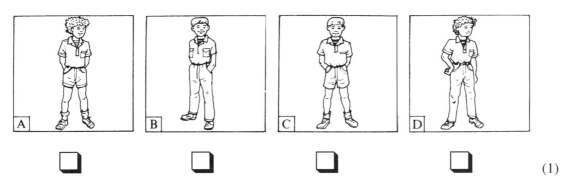

☐   ☐   ☐   ☐   (1)

2 Vous voulez aider à la maison. La mère de Jean-André vous dit:

Que vous demande-t-elle de faire?

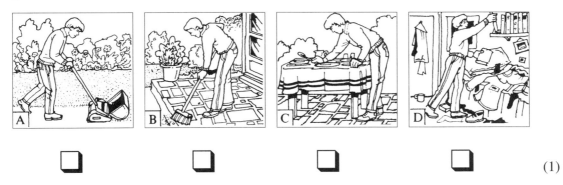

☐   ☐   ☐   ☐   (1)

3 Un autre soir, Jean-André et sa sœur, Michelle, parlent du week-end prochain.

Qu'est-ce que Michelle voudrait faire?

☐   ☐   ☐   ☐   (1)

UCLES 1995

23

TASK E

No box-ticking in this exercise, just answers to be written in French. The details are still brief, but be careful! This is a tricky exercise and you will need to listen carefully to both playings.

Vous passez vos vacances en France. Vous écoutez la radio et vous entendez une annonce sur les sorties à faire pendant les vacances.

Vous allez entendre l'annonce deux fois. Pendant que vous l'écoutez, remplissez les blancs et complétez les notes en français. Vous avez d'abord quelques secondes pour étudier les notes.

Poitiers

Activité/distraction: Cinéma 'Solido'

1   Dates: *du* .... *au* ....   (1)

2   Dans le cinéma il faut porter ....   (1)

Numéro de téléphone: | 4 | 9 | 4 | 9 | 3 | 0 | 1 | 0 |

La Rochelle

3   Activité/distraction: ....   (1)

Dates: du 13 au 18 août

4   Pays d'origine des artistes: (i) ....

(ii) *Antilles*

(iii) ....   (1)

Numéro de téléphone: | 4 | 6 | 5 | 0 | 5 | 6 | 3 | 9 |

Paris

Activité/distraction: Fête de la Forme

Date: dimanche 24 septembre

5   Prix de participation: ....   (1)

6   Moyens d'aller de la Tour Eiffel à Versailles:

(i) ....

(ii) ....   (1)

(iii) *vélo*

Boulogne-sur-Mer

Attraction du Centre Nausicaa: *ferme aquacole*

vidéos interactives

7   ....   (1)

8   Numéro de téléphone: | | | | | | | | | (1)

UCLES 1995

You will often be asked to listen to people talking about career plans. Here you have to pick out specific details and write them in the grid in French.

Ecoutez cette conversation entre Paul, Amélie et Marc, et remplissez la grille.

	Métier choisi	Raison du choix	Inconvénient
Paul			
Amélie			
Marc			

(9)

NEAB specimen

At this level, the pace of the French generally increases. There is a greater variety of voices and exercise types. The passages are usually longer and the vocabulary broader with varied tenses.

Although you are still required to listen for specific details, you are also asked to understand the general gist of what is being said, to consider the mood or emotion of the speakers and to draw conclusions from what you hear.

Answers written in French will be more complex, but remember that your standard of written French is NOT being tested here – it needs to be understandable to a French person. Give answers which provide all the details asked for by the questions, but don't worry about writing complete sentences.

You will generally find that you have to listen to both playings of the text. Don't worry if you don't understand it first time – make notes on what you understand and write your answers when you have listened again.

> Again, each exercise has only been recorded once on the CD but you would hear the text at least twice in the exam. The pauses during the texts have been recorded in full, but have been shortened at the end of each. Pause after each playing for 20–30 seconds while you write any answers you want to at this stage. Then recap to the start of the text, listen again carefully, pause at the end for a further 20–30 seconds and write the remaining answers.

To start with, a brief exercise in which you need to compare written details with what you hear and indicate the differences.

Ecoutez cette publicité. Puis regardez l'affiche, et **corrigez** les **trois** erreurs **en français**.

DISCOTHEQUE
la main jaune
ouvert aux moins de 18 ans

entrée 50F

bière.........10F
Coca Cola......5F

ouvert le weekend
de 14h à 19h

ERREUR

(3)

NEAB specimen

TASK H

In this exercise based on radio extracts you have to match up the content of each with a brief description.

Vous allez entendre six petits extraits de la radio française.

Regardez la liste des descriptions A à I.

Descriptions

A   événement à venir
B   émission de jeux
C   circulation routière
D   crime
E   bulletin de météo
F   émission musicale
G   publicité
H   sport
I   émission touristique

Écoutez les extraits et choisissez la description qui correspond le mieux à chaque extrait. Écrivez la lettre A, B, C, D, E, F, G, H ou I dans la case pour chaque question.

Description

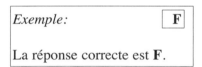

Exemple: **F**

La réponse correcte est **F**.

Et maintenant, à vous.

	Extrait	Description	
1	1	☐	(1)
2	2	☐	(1)
3	3	☐	(1)
4	4	☐	(1)
5	5	☐	(1)
6	6	☐	(1)

MEG specimen

Careful listening is required in this next exercise, in which you have to pick out the seven correct statements.

Vous allez entendre deux fois une conversation entre deux jeunes, Guillaume et Sophie.

Pendant que vous écoutez leur conversation, répondez aux questions en cochant la case **seulement si l'affirmation est vraie**. Il y a 7 affirmations vraies. Ne cochez pas **plus de 7 cases**. Vous avez d'abord quelques secondes pour lire les affirmations.

(a) Sophie est en pleine forme. ❑

(b) Il a fait mauvais samedi dernier. ❑

(c) Les parents de Guillaume ne regardent pas les matchs de football. ❑

(d) Le père de Sophie s'intéresse aux matchs de football. ❑

(e) Guillaume accompagne son petit frère aux matchs de football. ❑

(f) Sophie propose à Guillaume d'aller ensemble au prochain match. ❑

(g) Le père de Sophie ira voir les parents de Guillaume. ❑

(h) Guillaume a passé le week-end chez lui. ❑

(i) Les parents de Guillaume ont passé le week-end à la campagne. ❑

(j) Les cousins de Sophie ne vont pas en classe le samedi matin. ❑

(k) Les cousins de Sophie ont un peu moins de vacances qu'elle. ❑

(l) Guillaume préférerait aller à l'école le samedi matin. ❑ (7)

UCLES 1995

TASK J

Here is an example of an exercise in which you have to pick out opinions and attitudes.

Madame Duval, son fils Alain et sa fille Marie vont passer des vacances en Angleterre. Pour chaque phrase, coche ✔ la case de la personne (ou les personnes) qui exprime(nt) cette opinion.

		MME DUVAL	ALAIN	MARIE	
Exemple:	Dit que voyager par le Tunnel est confortable.			✔	
1	Dit qu'on ne voyage pas très vite si on prend le Tunnel.				(1)
2	Trouve qu'on devrait prendre le Tunnel parce que ce serait une nouvelle expérience.				(2)
3	Propose un autre moyen de transport.				(1)
4	Dit qu'il faut faire une comparaison des tarifs.				(1)

5   En conclusion, quelles sont leurs attitudes à ce sujet?
     Coche ✔ les trois bonnes cases.

	MME DUVAL	ALAIN	MARIE	
Est plutôt pour le Tunnel.				
N'a pas une opinion très forte à ce sujet.				
A peur de voyager sous la mer.				
Est plutôt contre le Tunnel.				(3)

ULEAC specimen

The previous three exercises have involved matching up and choosing alternatives, but you will also have to write answers in French. Here is an example which includes some multiple choice questions as well.

Vous allez entendre une conversation entre une jeune française, Marie-Jo, qui habite à Limoges et son frère, Marc. Marc a fait un voyage très difficile de Paris en voiture.

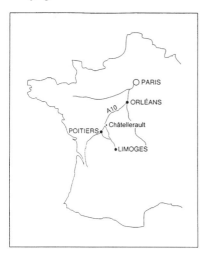

Regardez les questions 1 à 9.
Écoutez la conversation et répondez aux questions **en français**, ou cochez la case appropriée.

1 A quelle heure Marc a-t-il quitté Paris?

.... (1)

2 Pourquoi est-il rentré à son appartement?

.... (1)

3 Pourquoi a-t-il mis si longtemps pour regagner le périphérique?

.... (1)

4 Quel problème a-t-il eu vers dix heures?

.... (1)

5 Quand il s'est remis en route, Marc était:

(Cochez UNE case)   A – content. ☐

B – de mauvaise humeur. ☐

C– bête. ☐

D – très fatigué. ☐   (1)

6 Quel temps a-t-il fait à Orléans?

....

.... (2)

7 Expliquez ce qui s'est passé près de Châtellerault vers trois heures.

....

.... (1)

8 Nous avons l'impression que Marc:

(Cochez UNE case) A – conduit d'une façon dangereuse. ☐

B – est très nerveux. ☐

C– conduit sa voiture lentement. ☐

D – est un peu distrait. ☐ (1)

9 Quelle est l'attitude de Marie-Jo envers son frère?

(Cochez UNE case) A – Elle l'aime bien. ☐

B – Elle pense qu'il est bête. ☐

C – Elle est très fâchée contre lui. ☐

D – Elle le trouve amusant. ☐ (1)

MEG specimen

TASK L At least one of the Higher Tier exercises is likely to have questions in English for you to answer in English. Here you are tested on the skill of drawing a conclusion about a situation.

Two drivers discuss why the traffic has suddenly come to a halt.

(a) Why is driver A so upset?

....

.... (3)

(b) Who is causing the hold-up according to Driver B?

.... (1)

(c) What does he think these people should really be doing?

....

.... (3)

NICCEA 1994

REVISION HINTS

As in the Listening component, regular practice during the year leading up to the examination is the best revision device. Practise the exam questions in this book, then check your answers, noting where you went wrong, and read the examiner's tips carefully.

You need to learn vocabulary on a regular basis. You may well have vocabulary lists, either in a textbook, in a vocabulary revision guide or on lists given to you by your teacher. Look at these regularly, not aiming to do too much in any one session but working progressively through the separate topics.

There are various ways of trying to remember vocabulary – test yourself or ask a friend or relative to test you, copy the words down (writing them helps you to remember them) or read them through several times, putting a mark next to those that you find the most difficult to retain so that you can concentrate on those in particular. However it is always useful to try and use the words in speaking or writing, as soon as you can. By using the words in this way you will find that they 'stick' much more easily.

EXAMINATION HINTS

Many of the hints provided in the Listening section apply equally to the Reading exam. Obviously, as on the Listening paper, you need to check at all times that you are answering the questions set in a clear and legible way.

Even with those questions which you find easy, you should always take great care. At the same time, don't spend too long on any item which you find difficult. Come back to it later – but make a note that you have left it unanswered. The questions in the later sections will generally be more difficult and will require more time and care, but don't be in too much of a rush to start these questions until you are as sure as you can be that you have answered the easier sections correctly.

Do check that you have not missed anything. Many candidates each year turn two pages of the exam paper by mistake, or fail to turn over the final page.

You are allowed to use a dictionary in the Reading exam. As mentioned in the introductory section, you need to be selective in the words you look up. You must be careful not to spend too much time looking up words. Obviously it helps to know the alphabet really well so that you can find the meanings of those words that you do look up as quickly as possible (though of course taking care that you select the correct entry when more than one possible meaning is given).

Among the questions, there will be multiple-choice exercises, true/false items (*vrai* or *faux*), matching-up exercises (letters matched to statements, for example) and there is also likely to be one exercise with questions and answers in English. You will see examples of all these question types on the following pages.

You will also, however, have to write answers in French. Usually in Foundation Tier exercises of this type you will only have to write individual words. At Higher Tier you are likely to be required to write longer answers, though full sentences are not necessary.

Since the Reading exam is a test of your ability to understand French, however, you will not lose marks for inaccurate French. Your French has to be understandable to a French person with no knowledge of English.

At the same time, this does not necessarily mean that your answers can be brief. You should aim to answer the questions fully and reasonably accurately. Although you do not have to write full sentences, you should provide all the information required by the question. There are plenty of examples in the exercises which follow of what is required when answering questions in French.

> **If you need to revise this subject more thoroughly, see the relevant topics in the *Letts* GCSE French Study Guide.**

FOUNDATION

TASK A

To start you off, here is a simple exercise in which you have to match up items with the shops where they would be bought.

Voici une liste et un plan des magasins. Pour chaque produit indiquez avec une flèche le magasin où vous allez l'acheter.

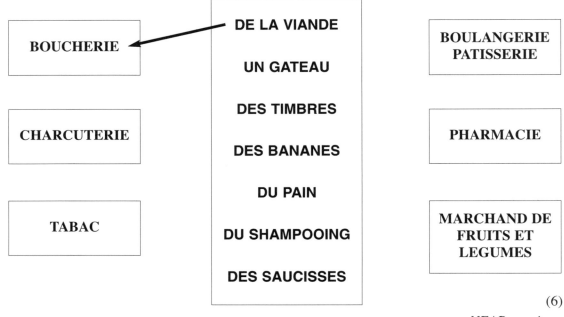

(6)

NEAB specimen

TASK B
Some of the simple exercises could have instructions in English. Here are three examples.

1 At a buffet they sell sandwiches.

SANDWICHES	
JAMBON	12 F 50
FROMAGE	11 F 00
SAUCISSON	13 F 00
POULET	14 F 00

How much is a ham sandwich?

A 12 F 50 ☐

B 11 F 00 ☐

C 13 F 00 ☐

D 14 F 00 ☐

(1)

MEG 1998

2 There is a sign:

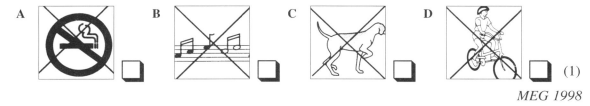

DÉFENSE DE FUMER

This means:

A ☐ B ☐ C ☐ D ☐ (1)

MEG 1998

3 You have a message from a French friend who will meet you at your destination.

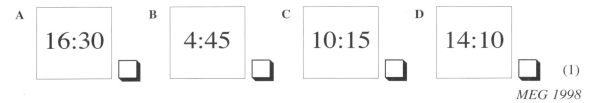

Je vais vous attendre dans le café à dix heures et quart.

What time are you expected to arrive at the café?

A 16:30 ☐ B 4:45 ☐ C 10:15 ☐ D 14:10 ☐ (1)

MEG 1998

The next example tests understanding of different places in the town. Although a little more reading in French is involved, the example makes it clear what is required.

TASK C

1 Regarde ces photos et **choisis une lettre** pour répondre aux questions.

A  B  C

D  E  F

Exemple: Où vas-tu pour acheter un timbre? .... *E* ....

(i)   Où vas-tu pour prendre un train? .... (1)

(ii) Où peux-tu lire des livres? .... (1)

(iii) Où peux-tu organiser les vacances? .... (1)

(iv) Où vas-tu si tu es malade? .... (1)

(v)   Où vas-tu pour parler avec un agent de police? .... (1)

WJEB 1998

TASK D The next two examples provide more material to read and they need to be done carefully.

1 Vous voulez aller au cinéma jeudi prochain avec des amis. A l'entrée, vous lisez les renseignements suivants:

CINEMA LUMIERE

Heures des séances: Salle 1, 2 & 3
Tous les jours: séance à 21 heures
Samedi: séances à 17 heures et 21 heures
Dimanche: matinée à 14 heures
séances à 17 heures et 21 heures

A quelle heure pouvez-vous y aller?

A ☐ 14.00   **B** ☐ 20.00

C ☐ 17.00   **D** ☐ 21.00   (1)

2 Vous voulez savoir quel temps il va faire demain. Vous cherchez dans le journal. A quelle page allez-vous?

NOS RUBRIQUES.
• COURSES (17 et 18) • ÉCONOMIE-SOCIAL-FINANCES (22) •
JEUX (2) • JOURNÉE (4) • LOISIRS (15 et 16) • MÉDECINE (8) •
MEDIA PUBLICITÉ (24) • MÉTÉOROLOGIE (14) • MOTS CROISÉS
(4) • NOTRE VIE (6 et 7) • PORTE OUVERTE CHEZ (20) • PETITES
ANNONCES (19 et 20) • RADIO-TÉLÉVISION (23 à 25) • RELIGION
(6) • SOLUTION DES JEUX (10) • SPECTACLES (21 et 22) • TAPIS
VERT (4) • VIE EN ÉTÉ (20) • VIE INTERNATIONALE (3 et 4) • VIE
POLITIQUE (5) • VIE SCIENTIFIQUE (8) • VIE SPORTIVE (11 à 13)

A ☐ Page 6

B ☐ Page 8

C ☐ Page 10

D ☐ Page 14   (1)

UCLES specimen

In this next exercise, you match signs with written instructions.

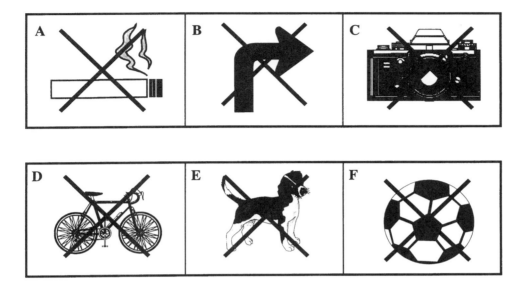

Écris la bonne lettre à côté de chaque phrase.

Exemple: Interdit de tourner à droite   B

(a) Défense de fumer   (1)

(b) Chiens interdits   (1)

(c) Défense de prendre des photos   (1)

ULEAC specimen

Reading exercises will sometimes be based on material such as messages, menus or letters. A different 'font' or handwriting may be used. In these first examples, you won't have any problems in deciphering the writing.

1 Vous êtes dans un restaurant. Vous ne mangez pas de viande. Quel plat choisissez-vous?

Côtes de Porc Forestière   A

Jambon sauce Madère   B

Gratin de légumes   C

Veau Marengo   D   (1)

2 Vous êtes chez des amis français. En rentrant, vous trouvez ce message:

> On va rentrer tard.
> Peux-tu acheter des boissons pour ce soir?
> Merci. A bientôt.

Que devez-vous acheter?

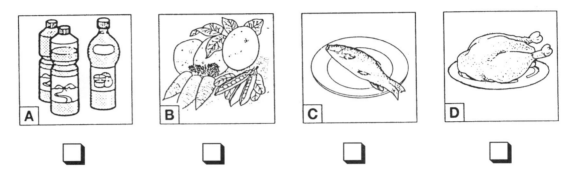

A ☐ B ☐ C ☐ D ☐

(1)

UCLES 1996

TASK G In this next example, the handwriting is a little more 'natural' and therefore rather more difficult to read.

Lisez la lettre.

Mardi, mon premier cours, à 8H30, c'est français! A 9H30 j'ai une heure d'anglais. A 10H30 il y a Sciences et à 11H30 j'ai une heure de Maths. L'après-midi à 2H j'ai encore une heure de Maths, et à 3H j'ai deux heures de dessin – ma matière préférée.

Complétez en français l'emploi du temps pour mardi.

	LUNDI	MARDI
8H30	MATHS	
9H30	FRANÇAIS	
10H30	ANGLAIS	
11H30	HISTOIRE _ GÉO	
	DÉJEUNER	
2H00	SCIENCES	
3H00	EPS	
4H00	EPS	

(7)

NEAB specimen

TASK H As a final exercise in this section, here is another example containing handwriting. You are required to show understanding of the comments on a school report.

Lisez le bulletin scolaire.

BULLETIN TRIMESTRIEL	Nom: Hubert	Prénom: Loïc
		Classe: 3ème B
Disciplines	**Appréciations**	
Français	Bien à l'oral mais ne fait jamais ses devoirs. Aucun effort.	
Anglais	Élève très impoli. Manque de respect.	
Mathématiques	Fait beaucoup d'efforts. Travail très sérieux.	
Histoire-Géographie	Parle trop avec ses voisins. N'écoute pas le cours.	
Sciences physiques	Un des meilleurs élèves de la classe.	
Dessin	Très calme - ne participe pas.	
Education physique et sportive	Ne fait aucun progrès - peu d'aptitude.	

Dans quel cours est-ce que Loïc montre les qualités suivantes?

Qualités	Cours
Exemple: Excellent	Sciences physiques
Faible	
Travailleur	
Insolent	
Paresseux	
Bavard	
Timide	

(6)

The increase in difficulty from Foundation to Higher Tier in Reading is similar to that in Listening. Texts are longer and more dense, extra topic areas are covered and more complex vocabulary and structures are tested. In addition, you are required to pick out important points and themes and to identify gist rather than simply show understanding of single words or short phrases. And, as in Listening, you have to identify attitudes, ideas and emotions and draw conclusions from what you read.

All this means that it is important to work slowly and carefully, to read texts thoroughly before answering the questions, to make judicious use of the dictionary and to take care to write answers that are clear, unambiguous and complete.

You will again have a variety of question types – matching, true/false, multiple choice, questions in English, questions in French and so on.

To start with, here is an example with questions in French. Re-read the examiner's tip given for Reading H.

Lisez cet lettre.

Salut!

Je suis très contente d'avoir une correspondante. J'aime beaucoup écrire. Voici une lettre pour me présenter.

J'ai quinze ans et j'habite à Bordeaux avec ma mère et mon petit frère. Mon frère aîné n'habite plus chez nous. Il s'est marié l'année dernière et lui et sa femme ont un appartement en ville.

J'ai une chambre pour moi seule que j'ai aménagée moi-même. A mon avis c'est très bien fait, mais tu me diras ce que tu en penses quand tu la verras. Dans ma chambre j'aime écouter ma musique, surtout les chansons d'amour.

J'aime beaucoup manger les choses sucrées comme les glaces et les desserts. J'en mange trop, je l'avoue. Cela agace ma mère qui se fait du souci à propos de ma santé.

J'ai beaucoup de copains et de copines et on se réunit souvent au café pour bavarder. J'aime ça. C'est plutôt le weekend car pendant la semaine il y a toujours beaucoup de devoirs à faire. Je les fais dans ma chambre, en écoutant la musique, bien sûr.

Cette année je suis allée en vacances d'été avec ma famille au bord de la mer. On s'est bien amusé, mais l'été prochain j'espère partir en bande avec mes copains dans les montagnes.

Au collège je suis assez forte en langues, mais en sciences et maths je suis nulle.

Je serai ravie de t'accueillir avec l'échange à Pâques. Écris-moi vite pour me renseigner sur tes goûts et tes intérêts. Je suis sûre qu'on s'amusera très bien ensemble.

A bientôt,

Céline

Exemple:

Céline, pourquoi est-ce qu'elle est contente?

$\underline{\text{Elle a une correspondante.}}$ ....

Répondez **en français**.

1   Céline, combien de frères a-t-elle?

.... (1)

2   Que pense-t-elle de sa chambre?

.... (1)

3 Pourquoi est-ce que sa mère s'inquiète pour sa fille?

.... (1)

4 Pourquoi est-ce qu'elle aime aller au café?

.... (1)

5 Où a-t-elle passé les grandes vacances?

.... (1)

6 Qu'est-ce qui se passera à Pâques?

.... (1)

MEG 1997

TASK J You are quite likely to have blank-filling exercises in which you select the missing words from a list. Having a good understanding of grammar helps with this type of test.

Tu lis cette lettre dans un magazine.

Le courrier des lecteurs

CHÈRE MIREILLE

Je m'appelle Corinne et je recherche un garçon que j'ai rencontré dans le train à destination de Paris, le 28 août dernier. Il est châtain, il a les yeux marron clair. Il mesure 1m70 environ. Il était vêtu d'un pantalon vert et d'une chemise blanche. Nous avons discuté un peu, mais je ne sais pas son nom. Si quelqu'un le connaît, montrez-lui mon message, s'il vous plaît, et dites-lui de m'appeler au (16.1) 325.28.16. Merci à tous.

Remplis les blancs pour donner le sens de la lettre. Choisis parmi les mots dans la case.

> s'appelle; hiver; été; bruns;
>
> blonds; téléphone; parlé, écrit;

Corinne a rencontré ce garçon l' ....dernier. Il a les cheveux ....

Corinne a ....un peu à ce garçon, mais elle ne sait pas comment il

.... Elle veut que le garçon lui .... (5)

ULEAC specimen

Next, an example of an exercise with questions in French and a multiple-choice question. The French seems a little complicated, but you should be able to find the answers fairly easily.

Vous avez reçu ces renseignements sur quelques vidéos en France.

VIDEO
La nouvelle année

● *La cité de la joie*, de Roland Joffé, adapté du best-seller de Dominique Lapierre. Un jeune chirurgien américain, joué par Patrick Swayze, donne un nouveau sens à sa vie en intégrant une équipe médicale au cœur de la misère des bidonvilles de Calcutta. Un film généreux. (Pathé/PCF Vidéo, 159 F.)

● *Cadence*. L'acteur Martin Sheen réalise ici son premier film, qu'il interprète face à son fils Charlie Sheen. L'action se situe dans l'univers disciplinaire d'une base militaire américaine, en Allemagne, rassemblant nombre de soldats noirs. Un vieux sergent et une nouvelle recrue s'affrontent. (UGC Vidéo. 159 F.)

● *Les quatre saisons du berger*, Cet excellent reportage signé Jean-Paul Jaud pour Canal + témoigne de la vie d'Alphonse, le berger des montagnes des Hautes-Pyrénées. Une existence en harmonie avec la nature. (Canal + Vidéo)

(a) Quel rôle Patrick Swayze a-t-il joué dans '**La cité de la joie**'?

.... (1)

(b) '**Cadence**' se situe dans quel pays?

.... (1)

(c) Qu'est-ce qu'Alphonse fait dans la vie dans '**Les quatre saisons du berger**'?

(i) il s'occupe de moutons. ☐

(ii) il est musicien. ☐

(iii) il est alpiniste. ☐ (1)

Cochez la bonne case.

NICCEA specimen

An interview now, again with questions in French.

Lis ce texte et réponds aux questions.

Laetitia Hubert a 18 ans. Elle est classée quatrième aux championnats du monde. Sophie Coucharrière l'a rencontrée au Palais Omnisports de Bercy, à Paris, juste après l'entraînement. Laetitia, en jeans et baskets, l'a gentiment reçue, dans les vestiaires, pour lui raconter sa vie de «tous les jours».

Sophie Coucharrière: *Comment tout cela a-t-il commencé pour vous?*

Laetitia Hubert: Mes parents aimaient beaucoup le patinage. Ils allaient à la patinoire, le week-end. Un jour, ils n'ont pas trouvé de nourrice pour me garder, ils ont été obligés de m'emmener. J'avais 3 ans, et très mauvais caractère, paraît-il!

Je leur ai fait une telle vie sur le bord de la piste, qu'ils ont fini par trouver des patins à ma taille, pour me faire patiner avec eux. Et au moment de partir, je ne voulais plus quitter la piste. Ils ont alors décidé de m'inscrire dans un club, une heure par semaine. Cela m'a plu, j'y suis allée, de plus en plus. Je suis entrée, à l'âge de 6 ans, dans une école de glace: l'École des enfants du spectacle, à Paris. C'est une école aménagée pour les sportifs, les musiciens, les acteurs, les danseurs, les élèves du cirque.

Sophie Coucharrière: *Alors, on vous verra peut-être aux Jeux Olympiques l'année prochaine?*

Laetitia Hubert: Malheureusement, non. Je suis maintenant professionnelle.

(i) Laetitia Hubert a quel âge?

.... (1)

(ii) Qu'est-ce qu'elle faisait juste avant cette interview?

.... (1)

(iii) Qu'est-ce qu'elle portait comme vêtements au moment de l'interview?

.... (2)

(iv) Elle a commencé à faire du patinage à quel âge?

.... (1)

(v) Comment était-elle quand elle était très petite? Coche (✔) la bonne case. (1)

gentille	méchante	sage	sympa

(vi) Comment sais-tu qu'elle aimait beaucoup le patinage comme enfant?

....

.... (2)

(vii) Pourquoi est-ce qu'elle n'ira pas aux Jeux Olympiques?

.... (1)

Now two examples of true/false exercises.

A l'entrée de l'autoroute on vous donne le prospectus suivant. Lisez-le attentivement, puis répondez aux questions en cochant la case **VRAI** ou **FAUX**.

L'AUTOROUTE PRATIQUE

LA SÉCURITÉ

L'autoroute est 4 à 5 fois plus sûre que la route. A chacun de la rendre encore plus sûre, en appliquant quelques règles faciles à respecter.

● Où s'arrêter? En cas de nécessité absolue, vous pouvez vous arrêter au bord de l'autoroute sur la bande d'arrêt d'urgence. Prenez le maximum de précautions car vous serez frôlé par les véhicules en circulation: stationnez donc le plus à droite possible.

● Attention à la fatigue. La conduite sur autoroute tend à vous endormir. Évitez ce risque en cassant la monotonie de votre

rythme de conduite et en modifiant votre vitesse et la température intérieure de votre voiture. N'hésitez pas à vous arrêter sur les parkings et les aires de repos environ toutes les deux heures.

LES SERVICES

Sur l'autoroute, vous trouverez des aires de repos tous les 10 à 15 km (avec points d'eau et toilettes), et tous les 30 à 40 km des aires de service où vous trouverez des stations services (avec boutiques), certaines étant équipées de cafétérias ou de restaurants.

© Autoroutes du Sud de la France

		VRAI	FAUX	
1	Les autoroutes sont plus dangereuses que les routes.	❏	❏	(1)
2	On peut s'arrêter au bord de l'autoroute pour se reposer.	❏	❏	(1)
3	Sur autoroute on risque de s'endormir au volant.	❏	❏	(1)
4	Il est conseillé de rouler à une vitesse constante.	❏	❏	(1)
5	Il est aussi conseillé de s'arrêter toutes les deux heures.	❏	❏	(1)
6	Sur les autoroutes, on trouve une station d'essence tous les 10 km.	❏	❏	(1)

UCLES 1995

The second example is more involved as you have to correct the false statements.

Lisez ce texte.

JEUNES
Une journée particulière

«Didier, saute plus haut, essaie d'attraper le ciel!» Sur son trampoline Didier rebondit comme un ballon. Ce matin, il a eu une bonne heure de vélo tout terrain. Tout à l'heure, il terminera l'après-midi par une initiation à l'équitation au centre hippique. Inutile de dire que lorsqu'il regagnera le domicile familial ce soir, Didier, comme ses copains, tombera de fatigue.

Vélo tout terrain, découverte de la nature, équitation, trampoline ... Ils seront deux mille au mois d'août à profiter du choix proposé par le conseil général du Nord. On

les reconnaît à leur tee-shirt illustré. «L'été des collégiens», c'est le nom de cette opération organisée par le département, une «première», destinée en priorité aux 12-16 ans qui ne partent pas en vacances.

Pendant des journées particulières, on essaie de marier l'utile et l'agréable.

Le circuit en VTT, par exemple, est l'occasion d'une découverte de la nature. Lecture d'une carte, utilisation d'une boussole pour s'orienter, informations sur la botanique et les rivières... On apprend sans s'ennuyer.

Pour cette opération organisée avec les villes et les associations des animateurs spécialisés sont mobilisés.

Les villes n'ont pas hésité: une journée aussi variée en activités pour une centaine de jeunes qui ne partent pas en vacances, voilà une chance qui ne se refuse pas.

L'opération «L'été des collégiens» devrait se répéter l'an prochain puisqu'elle a prouvé cette année que l'on peut trouver le dépaysement et la découverte sans aller à l'autre bout du monde.

Cochez la case VRAI si l'affirmation est vraie.
Cochez la case FAUX si l'affirmation est fausse puis corrigez l'affirmation.

Exemple	VRAI	FAUX
Affirmation		
Didier va pratiquer le trampoline toute la journée	☐	☑
Il va faire de l'équitation.		

Affirmation	VRAI	FAUX
1 Le conseil général du Nord organise toutes ces activités.	☐	☐
2 Cette opération s'appelle "Les journées particulières".	☐	☐
3 Tous les jeunes sans exception peuvent participer à ces journées.	☐	☐
4 Le seul objectif de ces journées c'est de pratiquer un sport.	☐	☐

....

5 Les participants peuvent avoir des vacances sans partir loin de chez eux.

❏ ❏

....

6 Cette opération sera supprimée l'an prochain.

❏ ❏

.... (10)

MEG specimen

TASK O

In the next exercise, you have to match short statements and questions to opinions given by three people.

Un magazine pour les jeunes a publié cet article.

UN AN À L'ÉTRANGER

Nous avons demandé à trois jeunes qui ont passé un an à l'étranger de nous donner leur opinion:

CAROLE: *Je me souviendrai toujours de mon premier jour aux Etats-Unis. On m'a réveillée à six heures. Il fallait prendre le bus à six heures et quart – même pas le temps de boire un café. Et puis une journée scolaire tout à fait différente. Je ne comprenais rien de ce qui se passait, c'était horrible – et puis le repas à la cantine était dégoûtant. Maintenant ça va un peu mieux, mais je ne m'y suis jamais vraiment habituée.*

JEAN-JACQUES: *Je me suis trouvé dans un petit village dans le North Dakota. La neige est tombée la deuxième semaine de septembre. J'ai eu très froid, et au début je me sentais un peu seul. Mais mes relations avec les autres se sont améliorées et j'ai trouvé l'ambiance du lycée très amicale.*

KARINE: *A la maison et au lycée on disait toujours que j'étais timide – mais en Australie j'ai fait des choses que je n'aurais jamais eu l'idée de faire en France. Du cross-country, alors que je ne suis pas du tout sportive! Je suis même devenue supporter de l'équipe de football...*

Pour chaque phrase ci-dessous, écris le nom de la personne qui a exprimé cette opinion.

(a) N'aimait pas le climat. .... (1)

(b) N'aimait pas la nourriture. .... (1)

(c) A essayé de nouvelles activités. .... (1)

(d) Devait se lever très tôt le matin. .... (1)

(e) Trouvait les autres élèves très accueillants. .... (1)

A ton avis,

(f) Qui a trouvé que son expérience avait du bon et du mauvais?

.... (1)

(g) Qui a trouvé l'expérience plutôt négative? .... (1)

(h) Qui a trouvé l'expérience positive? .... (1)

ULEAC specimen

TASK P Here is a similar exercise, but more difficult this time and with six separate texts to choose from.

Dans l'article suivant, des jeunes donnent leurs opinions sur les dessins, inscriptions (les 'graffiti') que l'on trouve partout aujourd'hui: sur les murs, dans les trains, les autobus.

POUR OU CONTRE?

Les graffiti: art ou vandalisme?

Sophie, 16 ans:
«Les graffiti font partie de la culture des jeunes d'aujourd'hui. C'est assez complexe, comme les autres formes d'art, mais c'est quand même une forme d'art pour des jeunes qui sentent qu'ils ont quelque chose à dire, et qui n'ont pas d'autre moyen de le dire.»

© Rex Features

Mathieu, 15 ans:
«Les graffiti, je trouve qu'on devrait les supprimer. Ça rend les grandes villes encore plus sales et plus moches. Quand tu montes dans un train ou dans un autobus, c'est dégoûtant de voir des graffiti sur les sièges.»

Pierre, 16 ans:
«Ceux qui font des graffiti, je crois qu'ils ont vraiment des problèmes. Savez-vous que des jeunes ont eu de graves accidents en esssyant d'écrire sur les rames de métro?»

Nicole, 17 ans:
«Les graffiti? Moi, ça m'est égal. Ça fait partie de la vie des grandes villes. Je suppose que c'est important pour les jeunes qui le font. C'est mieux de faire des graffiti que de se droguer ou voler. A mon avis, ça c'est beaucoup plus grave.»

Gilles, 16 ans:
«Je pense qu'il y a deux sortes de graffiti: il y a les graffiti faits n'importe comment sur les murs des stations de métro. Et puis il y a les graffiti qui ont une certaine valeur artistique. Il ne faut pas confondre les deux: les premiers, c'est du vandalisme et les seconds, c'est de l'art... peut-être. L'avenir le dira.»

Hélène, 14 ans:
«Les jeunes qui font des graffiti prennent cela très au sérieux. On dit qu'on va leur faire nettoyer les graffiti, au lieu de payer des amendes. Mais je pense que ce n'est pas une bonne idée. Je crois qu'il devrait y avoir des endroits où les jeunes créateurs de graffiti pourraient se rencontrer et développer leur art.»

Lisez les affirmations suivantes et répondez en écrivant dans la case appropriée la lettre qui correspond: **S** pour Sophie; **M** pour Mathieu; **P** pour Pierre; **N** pour Nicole; **G** pour Gilles; **H** pour Hélène.

1   Il est injuste de punir ceux qui font des graffiti. ☐ (1)

2   J'aimerais vivre dans une ville plus propre sans graffiti. ☐ (1)

3   Les graffiti sont le seul moyen d'expression des jeunes sans argent. ☐ (1)

4   Faire des graffiti peut être une activité dangereuse. ☐ (1)

5   Il y a des problèmes plus graves pour les jeunes que les graffiti. ☐ (1)

6   J'aimerais voir certains espaces réservés aux graffiti. ☐ (1)

UCLES 1995

As in the Listening, you are likely to have one or two exercises with questions and answers in English. Be prepared for the change of language! It is all too easy to overlook the instruction to write in English instead of French. As when writing answers in French, full sentences and long answers are not necessary.

   To finish off the Reading section, here are some exercises requiring the use of English.

TASK Q

You read this story about a couple's unfortunate start to married life.

Mariage ou sabotage?

Deux jeunes Français, Étienne et Marie-Laure, ne vont jamais oublier le "plus beau jour de leur vie":

– le frère du marié est tombé malade pendant la cérémonie, victime d'une insolation;

– la mariée a été prise d'une crise d'asthme;

– la voiture, qui emmenait le jeune couple à l'aéroport, a pris feu;

– enfin, on a cambriolé la maison des mariés…

– … et on leur a volé la vidéocassette de la cérémonie!

What happened to make the couple's wedding such a disaster? Mention any **four** things.

....

....

....

.... (4)

SEB 1996

While in France on holidays with your family, you decide to visit the tourist attraction 'Atlantic Toboggan'. You show your 9-year-old brother this brochure.

ATLANTIC TOBOGGAN

Une journée pas comme les autres, où pour le prix d'une entrée vous pourrez emprunter les toboggans de l'ouverture à la fermeture.

L'eau de toutes les attractions est constamment filtrée. Dans l'enceinte d'Atlantic Toboggan vous trouverez boissons fraîches, sandwiches, etc... Vous pourrez apprécier nos coins repos et apporter vos repas.

Prix d'entrée:
Adultes : 60F
Enfants 2 à 12 ans: 50F
Moins de 2 ans: GRATUIT.
Possibilité d'abonnements.
Tarif de groupe.
Réservation: Tél: 51 58 05 37 Parking.
5000 places **gratuites**.

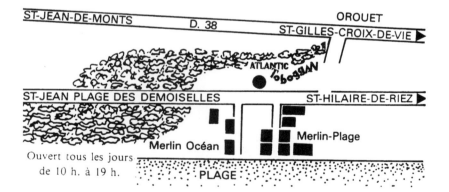

Your brother asks you these questions. Answer them in English.

(a) When is Atlantic Toboggan open?

.... (1)

(b) How much will it cost for me?

.... (1)

(c) Do we have to pay extra for the water chute?

.... (1)

(d) What's the water like?

.... (1)

(e) What will we do about food?

.... (1)

(f) What can we do if we get bored?

.... (1)

NEAB specimen

L'ex-rocker français se lance dans la politique japonaise

Claude Ciari est né à Nice en France. Mais l'année dernière, aux élections du Sénat japonais, il a obtenu près de 400 000 votes.

A 20 ans, Claude a fondé, avec des copains, un groupe rock, «Les Champions». Une de ses compositions, *la Playa*, a eu beaucoup de succès. «Un jour, j'ai appris qu'on vendait mes disques même au Japon! A ce moment-là, je ne savais même pas où ça se trouvait!»

C'était quand il faisait une tournée en Asie, que Claude a découvert le Japon. Il a immédiatement aimé le pays, et il est tombé amoureux de Yoshiko qu'il a épousée peu de temps après. «Je n'avais pas l'intention de vivre au Japon,» raconte Claude. «Nous sommes rentrés en France, mais Yoshiko ne se plaisait pas trop. Donc, on a décidé de s'installer définitivement au Japon.»

Aujourd'hui, Claude est directeur d'une importante compagnie d'informatique, il est aussi acteur, journaliste et musicien – il donne toujours 80 concerts annuels. Mais il trouve quand même le temps de faire de la politique. «On a une image déformée du Japon,» dit Claude. «Ce que l'on ne sait pas assez, c'est qu'il y a encore des gens qui meurent de faim et de froid. C'est pour ça que je veux faire de la politique.»

«J'adore toujours la France», précise Claude, «mais je n'ai pas l'impression de rentrer chez moi quand j'y retourne. Maintenant je suis japonais à 100%.»

(a) What surprising feat did this Frenchman achieve last year?

.... (1)

(b) How did Claude Ciari first become aware of Japan?

.... (1)

(c) What happened on his first visit there?

.... (1)

(d) Why did he decide to set up home in Japan?

.... (1)

(e) Why did Claude decide to become involved in politics?

.... (1)

(f) How has his attitude towards France changed?

.... (1)

SEB 1995

TASK T   Read this article.

> ## C'EST LE FACTEUR!
>
> Facteur? Factrice? Plutôt factrice puisque les femmes sont majoritaires dans cette profession qui n'a pourtant été féminisée qu'en 1975.
>
> À 34 ans Nadine est satisfaite de son emploi. Elle aime porter l'uniforme bleu marine qui est si bien connu partout en France. Cet uniforme est nécessaire parce que les personnes âgées surtout se méfient de plus en plus de ceux qui se présentent devant leur porte.
>
> C'est cette proximité quotidienne, cette confiance des autres, qui confortent Nadine dans son métier. Elle dit, "J'aime la communication et les rencontres et cela m'a amenée à aider les personnes âgées."
>
> Nadine ne pense pourtant pas exercer ce métier toute sa vie. "En dépit des joies de la communication, il y a la fatigue qui s'accumule. "Fatigue de se lever tous les jours à cinq heures et demie et de porter un sac très lourd. Surtout la fatigue due aux clients maussades. "Sur nous toutes les plaintes: si l'on a cinq minutes de retard par exemple. Et quelquefois, si une lettre attendue n'est pas arrivée, l'amoureux déçu accuse plus volontiers le facteur que sa partenaire inconstante!"
>
> Malgré les inconvénients, Nadine aime son travail "... qui permet d'être indépendant, de n'avoir personne derrière soi, de prendre le temps de bavarder,

de connaître chacun par son nom."

Certains jours sont plus éprouvants que d'autres. En particulier le jeudi, jour de distribution de nombreuses revues hebdomadaires qui pèsent lourd sur l'épaule.

Nadine dit. "Les horaires et le travail n'autorisent pas les soirées tardives entre amis."

Pour cette raison, nombreux sont les facteurs qui épousent des factrices!

Answer the following questions in **English**.

Example: What change did the French postal service introduce in 1975?

They appointed postwomen.

1   Why is it important for the postman or woman to wear a uniform?

.... (1)

2   Give **two** reasons why some people complain to the postman or woman.

(a) .... (1)

(b) .... (1)

3   Why do postmen often marry postwomen?

....

.... (1)

4   Which of the following most accurately summarises what Nadine says about her job?
   (Tick **one** only)

A   She likes her work and does not intend to change.   ☐

B   It is satisfying work but it is physically very demanding.   ☐

C   She thinks the drawbacks of her job outweigh the advantages.   ☐

D   She would rather not work on Thursdays.   ☐   (1)

MEG 1998

REVISION HINTS

Writing is the most demanding of the skill areas in French but, as with the other skills, regular careful revision and practice provide the key to success. The same hints regarding the learning of vocabulary mentioned in the Reading hints apply to writing. At the same time, you need to revise the basic points of French grammar regularly. You may have a textbook that provides a grammar summary at the back. Use it, but don't attempt to do too much at a time and remember to ask your teacher about anything that is not clear.

Pay particular attention to verbs – especially the irregular ones. You don't need to learn every part of every verb in the book – you wouldn't need them all and you probably wouldn't be able to learn them all. Concentrate on the first and third persons of the verb in the singular (*je* and *il/elle*) and in the plural (*nous* and *ils/elles*). Concentrate on the present tense, the perfect tense and the future tense, remembering that you can form a future tense by using the verb *aller* (to go) followed by the infinitive of the verb required (e.g. *je vais partir* – 'I'm going to leave'). Remember that at Higher Tier, you will also need to be able to form and use the imperfect tense properly. See the introduction for some further details on the tenses.

Practise the exercises in this book and read the accompanying commentaries. Remember too that the more you practise speaking French the easier you will find the other skills. Similarly, reading French will help your writing skills.

EXAMINATION HINTS

On the Foundation Tier papers, the important thing is to convey the message. Spelling has to be accurate enough to be understood by a French person, but you will not lose many marks for spelling errors. Check, then, that you have made the message clear, and that you have conveyed all the information required. You may be able to get round an idea even if you do not know a particular word – for example *sept jours* is a perfectly good alternative for 'a week' if you have forgotten the word *une semaine*.

On the Higher Tier papers, accuracy is much more important. Obviously you need to convey the message, and again you must be sure to include all the details asked for (tick them off on the paper as you do them) but then you must check for accuracy. If writing the past tense, have you included the part of *avoir* or *être* and have you included the right accent where it is required (e.g. *j'ai mangé*)? If you have written a plural, have you added the *s* to the noun and any adjective with it (e.g. *j'ai deux petits chiens*)? Re-read your work and look for errors and again, always ask yourself 'Is my writing clear enough to be read by the examiner and have I made any changes clear?' Try to recall the sort of errors you have made previously when writing French in an attempt to avoid making them again. Apart from accents and plural endings mentioned above, try to avoid those common spelling errors that so many candidates make with such words as *beaucoup de/d'*; *mercredi*; *le petit déjeuner*; *sœur*, etc. and remember the difference between *chevaux* and *cheveux*, *vieille* and *la veille*, *mois* and *moins*, etc.

Be prudent in your use of the dictionary. Remember that you will not have time to check each word, so use your dictionary as appropriate to find a particular word or to check spelling, the gender of a noun, etc. Whatever you do, don't run out of time through having spent too long checking words that you are fairly sure are correct. At the same time, it would be wise, if you have any time left after you finish your letter or essay, to make use of the dictionary to check spellings, genders and so on. In other words, don't waste time after you have finished writing by missing the opportunity to use your dictionary. Remember that everyone else has a dictionary and will be making use of it.

Because it is likely, when checking, that you will make changes to what you have written, it is a good idea to write on every second line of your answer paper. In this way you will be able to make any changes perfectly clear to the examiner by crossing through your first attempt and writing in your revisions neatly on the line above. It is probably better to follow this device rather than writing all the letter or essay in rough and then copying it up 'in neat'; this is time-consuming and it is not uncommon for candidates to mis-copy or to omit words as they write up a second version.

If you need to revise this subject more thoroughly, see the relevant topics in the *Letts* GCSE *French Study Guide*.

WRITING TASKS: PART 1 – SAMPLE QUESTIONS & ANSWERS

This section of the book is in two parts.

In the first part you will see some sample examination questions with suggested answers. In most cases the answers given are good, but they do contain a few errors, marked with a *. See if you can work out what the error is before referring to the commentary following each exercise.

In the second part, which starts on page 62, you will find practice questions for you to try yourself. There are no sample answers given to these, but you will find some hints as to how you might tackle the questions.

The early exercises at Foundation Tier often require you to write no more than individual words. Here is a very simple example to start you off.

FOUNDATION

You are going on a picnic with some French friends. Write a shopping list in FRENCH of THREE things to eat and ONE drink to take on the picnic.

TASK A

NEAB specimen

pain	limonade
tomates	
jambon	

ANSWER

Examiner's commentary Instructions for written exercises, even at Foundation Tier, will usually be given in French. In this type of exercise keep it simple, using words which you know are correct and which you do not therefore need to check in the dictionary. Try to avoid words which are exactly the same as in English, such as *oranges*. If you wrote 'lemonade' rather than the French *limonade* you would probably not be awarded the mark, even if you could argue that a French person would understand it.

TASK B

You will usually need to write rather more than four words, of course. Here is another example in which, although there is more to write, it is again acceptable to write individual words or details rather than sentences.

Remplissez ce formulaire EN FRANÇAIS avec vos détails personnels.

Demande pour Correspondant/e Français/e

À REMPLIR EN FRANÇAIS

NOM ET PRÉNOM: ....

NATIONALITÉ: .... (1)

ÂGE: .... (1)

DATE DE NAISSANCE: le ....19.......... (1)

COULEUR DES CHEVEUX: .... (1)

COULEUR DES YEUX: .... (1)

FAMILLE (FRÈRES ET SŒURS): ....

.... (1)

SPORT PRÉFÉRÉ: .... (1)

AUTRES INTÉRÊTS: (i)................................ (1)

(ii) .... (1)

MATIÈRE D'ÉCOLE FAVORITE: .... (1)

MEG specimen

ANSWER

À REMPLIR EN FRANÇAIS

NOM ET PRÉNOM: ..SMITH JANE..............

NATIONALITÉ: ..anglais*..................

ÂGE: ..15 ans..................

DATE DE NAISSANCE: le ..premier octobre 1982......

COULEUR DES CHEVEUX: ..bruns..........

COULEUR DES YEUX: ..blue*..........

FAMILLE (FRÈRES ET SŒURS): ..un frère..........
je n'ai pas de sœurs..................

SPORT PRÉFÉRÉ: ..tennis..........

AUTRES INTÉRÊTS: (i)..cinéma..........

(ii) ....*..........

MATIÈRE D'ÉCOLE FAVORITE: ..l'anglais..........

Examiner's commentary The candidate has correctly placed her surname before her first name – though you will notice that no marks are awarded for this first answer. The other details are all understandable, but one mark has been dropped for writing only one interest. Also, there would be no mark for 'blue'. *Bleu* would have been acceptable, though strictly speaking this should have been written *bleus* to agree with the plural word *yeux*. Similarly *anglaise* should have been written for *nationalité*. No marks are lost for writing the figure 15 rather than the word *quinze*, but it is good to add the word *ans* – remember that this must always be used when referring to one's age.

After the simple one-word or form-filling exercises, you will be asked to write a few simple sentences. An example will normally be given and you should study this carefully before writing your answers, though you should try to vary the structures as in this example.

Qu'est-ce qu'il y a à faire dans ton village ou ta ville?

Remplis cette fiche

Exemple   (i) On peut aller à la piscine

(ii) ....

(iii) ....

(iv) ....

(v) ....

(vi) ....

WJEC specimen

(ii) ...On peut aller à la discothèque....................

(iii) ...On peut visite* le musée..............................

(iv) ...On peut promenade* dans le parc.................

(v) ...On peut jouer au football..............................

(vi) ...On peut regarder un film à le* cinéma..........

Examiner's commentary   A good variety of verbs and a good standard of accuracy. *On peut* has been repeated each time to introduce each sentence, but it should always be followed by a verb in the infinitive. *There are three errors here. In (iii), it should be *visiter* (the infinitive) instead of *visite*. In (iv) *faire une promenade*. And in (vi) remember that *à + le* changes to *au*.

TASK D

You are often asked to write messages. Again, it is not always necessary to write in sentences, but it is better to do so. There will normally be five or so separate answers required, with the instructions written in French. Tick each task off as you do it. Here is a sample question and answer of this type.

Tu vas en ville.

Écris un message (environ 30 mots) à ton ami(e) pour dire:

● où tu vas   ● pourquoi

● avec qui   ● comment tu vas rentrer   ● à quelle heure tu vas rentrer

```
...................................................................................................
...................................................................................................
...................................................................................................
...................................................................................................
...................................................................................................
...................................................................................................
...................................................................................................
...................................................................................................
```

ULEAC
specimen

ANSWER

Je vais en ville pour acheter les provisions. J'y vais avec Robert. Je vais rentrer en autobus à cinq heures et demi*.

Examiner's commentary This is a good answer with just one error. Notice how the answers have been combined (e.g. transport and time in the last sentence). Notice too how important it is to be certain of the meanings of the different question words. *The only error is in the spelling of *demie* – the word must always be spelt with an *e* in times, as *heure* is a feminine word. However, with *midi* and *minuit* (which are both masculine), it is spelt *demi*.

Moving on now to more extended writing, several Examination Boards set the task of writing a postcard in French. Again, there will usually be five questions, explained in French and sometimes (as in this next example) with picture support.

Ma maison

Ecrivez une carte postale **en français:** maximum **40 mots.**

Exemples

– **où** habitez-vous?

– **quelle sorte** de maison avez-vous?

– vous avez **quelles pièces?**

– comment est **votre chambre?**

– **quels animaux** avez-vous?

MEG 1997

Cher Ami,
J'habite dans un petit village. J'habite dans une grand* maison à deux étages. Il y a un salon, une cuisine, une salle à manger et quatre chambre*. Dans mon* chambre j'ai une table et un ordinateur. Nous avons un chat.
Au revoir,
John.

Examiner's commentary Another good answer, covering each task fully and generally accurately and of about the right length. There is a suitable start and finish to the card. The candidate has dealt carefully with each detail. Note the good expression *maison à deux étages*. Note also how for the last task the phrase *nous avons* has been used to give a little variation from using *j'ai* and *il y a*.
* There are three errors of a type that you should try to avoid: it should be *une grande maison* (add "e" to the adjective when it goes with a feminine noun like *maison*); *chambre* here should have an "s" for the plural, as in English; finally, remember that it should be *ma chambre* as the word *chambre* is a feminine noun.

HIGHER

Usually at the Higher Tier you will be required to write a letter in French. You are generally asked to write between 100 and 150 words, though the number of words isn't as important as including all the points or answering all the questions – usually five or six.

Letters can be either informal (typically, to a French pen-friend) or formal (such as booking a hotel room, applying for a job, etc.). You must learn the appropriate phrases for starting and finishing letters of each type (you will see examples of each in the samples below).

Remember also that you must use the *vous* form of address in writing formal letters whereas, in writing to a pen-friend, the *tu* form will be more appropriate. However, if you are writing to the pen-friend's family, you would of course have to use *vous* as you are addressing more than one person.

TASK F

Here first is an example of an informal letter.

Vous avez reçu une lettre de votre correspondante française, Séverine.

Lisez sa lettre, puis écrivez une réponse **en français**. Répondez à toutes ses questions. **Ecrivez 100 mots.**

Toulouse, le 3 mai

Salut!

C'est Séverine, ton amie française! Je vais très bien. Tu vas bien aussi, j'espère.

Tu sais, j'ai un petit lapin maintenant! C'est maman qui me l'a donné comme cadeau d'anniversaire. Il est tout blanc et il est mignon! Est-ce que tu as des animaux domestiques? Comment sont-ils?

A l'école, ça va assez bien. J'aime bien l'anglais et l'histoire mais il y a des matières que je n'aime pas du tout comme les maths. Et toi? Quelles sont les matières que tu aimes et que tu n'aimes pas – et pourquoi?

J'ai passé un week-end superbe, le week-end dernier. Je suis allée à une boum chez mon amie Marie-Line. J'ai dansé et je me suis bien amusée. Qu'est-ce que tu as fait le week-end dernier?

Pendant les vacances d'été cette année je vais aller au bord de la mer. Mais je resterai à la maison au mois de juillet. Qu'est-ce que tu vas faire pendant les vacances? Est-ce que tu voudrais venir chez moi pour une semaine en juillet? J'espère que ce sera possible.

Ecris-moi vite pour répondre à toutes mes questions!

Amicalement,

Séverine.

MEG specimen

ANSWER

Chère Séverine,

Merci bien de ta lettre que j'ai reçue hier. Elle m'a fait grand plaisir. Moi aussi, je vais très bien.

Maintenant je vais répondre* tes questions.

Comme animaux domestiques nous avons un grand chien noir. Il s'appelle Rex et il est formidable!

A l'école j'aime surtout le français et l'histoire. Je n'aime pas beaucoup l'éducation physique – je ne suis pas sportive!

Le week-end dernier je suis allé* en ville avec mes amis. J'ai acheté un CD de Peter André.

Pendant les vacances je voudrais bien te visiter* en France. Merci bien!

Maintenant je dois terminer ma lettre.

Écris-moi bientôt,

Anne

This is an excellent answer with virtually no errors. Note particularly how the candidate:

- has used an accurate, appropriate start and finish to the letter;
- has answered all Séverine's questions in simple but accurate French;
- has clearly mastered verbs in French, using both present and past tenses confidently.

* The only errors are: the verb 'to answer' is *répondre à*; as it is a girl writing, she should have written *je suis allée*; when visiting a friend, you should use *rendre visite à*, not *visiter*.

Now study this formal letter, based on the common topic of booking a room in a hotel.

TASK G

Ecrivez une lettre **en français** pour réserver des chambres dans un hôtel à Calais.

Donnez des renseignements sur:

    (a) les chambres que vous désirez.

    (b) les dates de votre visite.

    (c) les repas que vous voudriez prendre.

Posez des questions sur:

    (a) le prix des chambres.

    (b) ce qu'il y a à l'hôtel (piscine? discothèque?)

    (c) l'endroit où l'hôtel est situé (centre-ville? près du port?)

ANSWER

> Stafford, le 10 octobre
>
> Madame/Monsieur,
>
> Je vous écris pour réserver des chambres dans votre hôtel. Je voudrais réserver deux chambres avec douche pour deux personnes. Nous voudrions rester une semaine, du premier au huit juillet, l'année prochaine. Nous voudrions aussi prendre le petit déjeuner à l'hôtel. Est-ce que c'est possible?
> Quels sont les tarifs? Est-ce qu'il y a une piscine à l'hôtel? Est-ce qu'il y a un ascenseur?
> Finalement, où se trouve l'hôtel? Est-il au centre-ville ou en banlieue?
> En attendant votre réponse, je vous prie d'agréer, Madame, Monsieur, l'expression de mes sentiments distingués.
>
> Elizabeth Jones

> **Examiner's commentary** This is another very well-written letter with no errors. Again notice how the candidate:
> • has provided a suitable start and finish to a formal letter (learn the special formula to finish such a letter);
> • has covered all the points required;
> • knows how to ask questions, by using question words and phrases such as *où* or *est-ce qu'il y a*;
> • has learned the useful phrase *Quels sont les tarifs?*, meaning 'How much do you charge?';
> • knows how to express dates covering a period of time *(du premier au huit)*. You can also use *à partir du premier ... jusqu'au huit.*

TASK H It is now quite common for Examination Boards to set writing tasks which involve applying for a job in France or French-speaking countries. Study this example and the specimen answer given.

Vous voulez perfectionner votre français. On vous propose de travailler dans une de ces compagnies:

1   Agence de voyages 'FRANCE-VOYAGES' (employé(e))

2   AIR-FRANCE (chef)

3   MICHELIN (Mécanicien/Mécanicienne)

Ecrivez une lettre EN FRANÇAIS à la compagnie de votre choix.

Parlez:

- de vos passe-temps
- de vos qualités personnelles
- de vos études en français
- des emplois que vous avez déjà faits (par exemple le baby-sitting, la distribution des journaux, un petit emploi dans un magasin, un stage en entreprise)
- Dites pourquoi cet emploi vous intéresse
- Dites pour combien de temps vous pourrez travailler

Demandez:

- les heures de travail
- le salaire
- des détails sur les repas

NEAB specimen

Birmingham, le 2 février   ANSWER

Madame/Monsieur,

Je vous écris pour demander du travail comme chef pour Air France. J'aime bien faire du sport et lire des romans et les journaux. Je suis intelligent, je travaille bien et j'ai beaucoup de patience. J'étudie le français depuis cinq ans et je parle aussi un peu l'espagnol. J'ai déjà travaillé en Angleterre. Quand j'avais douze ans, je distribuais les journaux et l'été dernier j'ai travaillé à temps partiel dans un petit magasin à Birmingham.

Je voudrais travailler comme chef pour Air France parce que je m'intéresse beaucoup aux avions et j'adore la cuisine! Je pourrez* travailler l'été prochain pendant six semaines à partir du vingt juillet.

Je voudrais vous poser quelques questions sur le travail. D'abord, à quelle heure commence et finit le travail? Ensuite, quel est le salaire? Et finalement, pouvez-vous me dire si vous donnez un déjeuner gratuit à vos employés?

Dans l'attente de recevoir bientôt votre réponse, veuillez agréer, Madame/Monsieur, l'expression de mes meilleurs sentiments.

Paul Davis

Examiner's commentary   This is a demanding exercise, requiring a lot of information. Note the following points arising from the sample answer:
- each point is taken in turn and dealt with simply but fully;
- the use of *j'étudie... depuis* for 'I have been studying... for'; remember to use the present tense if the learning is still going on;
- the use of the perfect and imperfect tense to describe jobs which have been done or used to be done;
- the different ways of asking questions in the last main paragraph;
- the appropriate ending to the letter.
* There is only one error – beware of taking a verb from the information and not making the necessary change to the ending – this should be *je pourrai*.

At Higher Tier, writing exercises very often ask you to express your opinions, your impressions and your reactions to events. Here is an example. In this case, the answer would not receive a good mark. Try to work out why not and see if you can correct the errors.   TASK I

Ecrivez 150 mots.

Vous avez passé récemment un week-end idéal avec votre famille ou vos amis.

Ecrivez une lettre à votre ami(e) français(e) pour raconter ce que vous avez fait pendant ce weekend. Parlez de vos impressions et expliquez pourquoi c'était le week-end idéal.

MEG specimen

le 25 juin 1995

Merci bien pour ta dernière lettre. Nous allons tous bien merci. J'espère que tu vais* bien, et ta famille aussi. La semaine dernière j'ai passe* un week-end idéal avec ma famille.

Nous sommes allé* au bord de la mer en voiture. Nous sommes partis* la maison à huit heures. Il faisait très chaud. Le voyage a duré environ trois heures. J'ai joué le* football sur la plage avec mon frère. J'ai mangé une glace au chocolat. C'était bien.

Nous avons visité la ville. J'ai acheté un chapeau au magasin. Nous sommes allés au restaurant pour mangé* le fish and chips*. C'était délicieux.

A sept heures nous avons rentré* à la maison. J'étais très fatigué. Je me couche* à dix heures. C'était un bon jour* et c'était idéal parce que j'aime la plage.

Examiner's commentary   At Higher Tier, a good degree of accuracy is expected. Credit is given for varied vocabulary and use of 'idiom' – phrases that sound typically French and add interest to the writing. It is also vital to follow instructions. The above example would not obtain a good mark because, apart from the errors and the lack of idiomatic French, very few impressions are given and there is little attempt to explain why it was an ideal weekend.
* Did you find out what was wrong with each of these?

- *Tu vas* – change the ending from *je vais*. The candidate has, however, remembered that when saying how you feel, the verb *aller* and not *être* must be used.
- *J'ai passé* – don't forget to include this accent which indicates the past participle.
- *Nous sommes allés* – verbs taking *être* in the perfect tense must agree with the subject – i.e. add an *s* for the plural.
- Verbs taking *être* must not be followed by an object. Hence you need either *nous avons quitté la maison* or *nous sommes partis **de** la maison*.
- *J'ai joué au football*.
- *Pour* meaning 'in order to' takes the infinitive – *pour manger*.
- Even if fish and chips is a typically English dish, you should always avoid writing it in English.
- *Rentrer* takes *être* – hence *nous sommes rentrés*.
- This should also be in the perfect tense – *je me suis couché*.
- It is better to use the word *journée* when describing a day – hence *une bonne journée*.

PART 2: PRACTICE QUESTIONS

Here are some writing exercises for you to practise. They match fairly closely the style of questions you have seen in Part 1, so it may help to have another look at the corresponding exercise in the first half before attempting each of these.

Vous allez dans un café avec quatre amis. Écrivez une liste de cinq boissons et de cinq choses à manger. Ecrivez en français.

	A boire		**A manger**
Exemple:	thé	Exemple:	sandwich au jambon

A boire	A manger
1.	1. ....
2.	2. ....
3.	3. ....
4.	4. ....
5.	5. ....

TASK K

Tu as lu cette annonce dans un magazine français.

ELEVES

Ecrivez-nous!

Nous avons besoin de renseignments sur vous!

- Nom

- Age

- Matière préférée au collège. Pourquoi?

- Passe-temps préférés

- Ambitions

Ecris ta réponse (environ 30 mots) à cette annonce.

Je m'appelle ....

....

....

....

....

....

.... (10)

Edexcel 1998

TASK L

Organisez votre visite en France!

Écrivez, **en français**, UNE ACTIVITÉ DIFFÉRENTE, pour chaque jour de votre visite.

	JOUR	ACTIVITÉ
exemple:	dimanche	je voudrais voir mes amis
exemple:	lundi	je voudrais aller à la piscine
	mardi	....(2)
	mercredi	....(2)
	jeudi	....(2)
	vendredi	....(2)
	samedi	....(2)

MEG specimen

Examiner's commentary | With two marks available for each activity, it obviously makes sense to write a little more than simply *cinéma* or *match de football*. Follow the pattern of the examples given by trying to include a verb with each one.

TASK M

Tu es en France chez ton/ta correspondant(e).

Tu sors un jour et tu laisses un message.

Écris un message en français pour dire

- où tu es allé(e)

Exemples

- comment tu y vas

- ce que tu vas faire

- à quelle heure tu vas rentrer

- ce que tu as fait avant de partir

Examiner's commentary Watch for the different tenses, but remember that, as this is a message written before going out, you could use either the present, past or future for the first three points. There would be no such choice, however, for the final two points.

Vous laissez un message en **français** pour votre copain/copine.
Choisissez un détail pour remplir chaque blanc.

TASK N

Exemple:

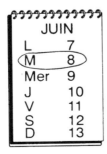

JUIN
L	7
M	8
Mer	9
J	10
V	11
S	12
D	13

C'est .... *mardi le 8 juin.* ......

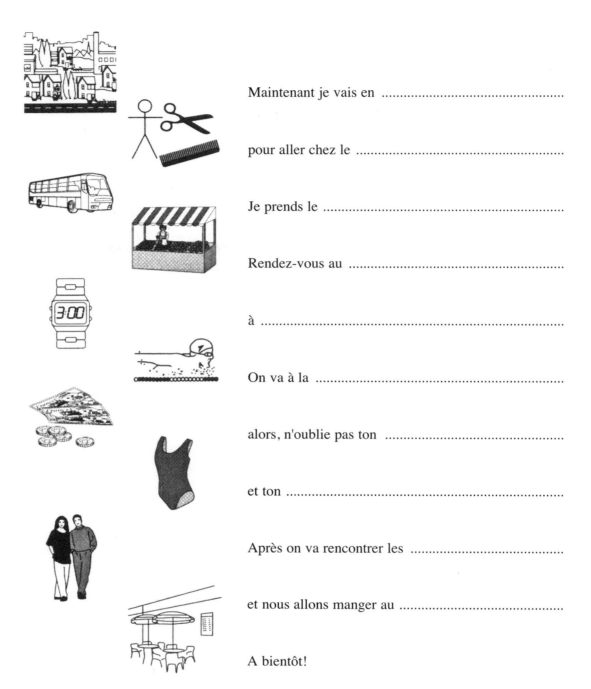

Maintenant je vais en ....

pour aller chez le ....

Je prends le ....

Rendez-vous au ....

à ....

On va à la ....

alors, n'oublie pas ton ....

et ton ....

Après on va rencontrer les ....

et nous allons manger au ....

A bientôt!

MEG 1998

Examiner's commentary   Much of the work has already been done for you here! You simply need to complete the sentences. You shouldn't even need to use the dictionary much.

Vous avez reçu une lettre de votre nouveau correspondant français, Luc.

Lisez sa lettre, puis écrivez une réponse en français. Répondez à toutes les questions. Ecrivez 100 mots.

Lyon, le 18 mars.

Salut!

Je suis ton nouveau correspondant français. Mon professeur m'a donné ton adresse.

Je m'appelle Luc et j'ai quinze ans. Dans ma famille nous sommes cinq (j'ai une sœur). Il y a combien de personnes dans ta famille et combien de frères et de sœurs as-tu?

J'habite à Lyon. C'est une très grande ville et ce n'est pas loin de la Suisse. Je l'aime bien, Lyon. Et toi, comment est ta ville? Qu'est-ce qu'il y a à faire dans ta ville?

J'adore lire. Je lis des romans, des bandes dessinées, des magazines - tout! Qu'est-ce que tu aimes faire, toi? Quel est ton passe-temps favori?

J'aime bien voyager avec ma famille. L'année dernière, au mois d'août, on est allé au Portugal. C'était très bien, mais il a fait si, si chaud! Qu'est-ce que tu as fait pendant les grandes vacances l'an dernier?

L'école, c'est pas mal. Quand je quitterai l'école je voudrais travailler pour la radio ou la télévision. Qu'est-ce que tu feras plus tard, toi?

Je dois terminer ma lettre maintenant. Ecris-moi vite et réponds à toutes mes questions!

Bien amicalement,

Luc.

MEG specimen

Examiner's commentary Spend some time finding the questions in the letter that need to be answered. Each short paragraph ends with a question requiring an answer. Notice also that you have to use present, past and future tenses. Don't forget to include a suitable beginning and end.

Regardez cette annonce pour un emploi en Suisse.

ON RECHERCHE

Jeunes gens ou jeunes filles

pour travailler dans notre

CAFÉ/RESTAURANT

Si cela vous intéresse, écrivez au patron:

M. Martin, 128 Rue de Lausanne, Genève, Suisse

Vous voudriez travailler dans ce café/restaurant.

Ecrivez une lettre de candidature de 120 à 150 mots. Dans la lettre, donnez:

- des renseignements sur vous
- vos qualités
- votre expérience du travail

et posez des questions sur:

- les horaires de travail
- le salaire

Examiner's commentary In asking questions about hours and pay, it is useful to know the phrase *Je voudrais savoir...* meaning 'I would like to know...'. Add appropriate words such as *si* (if), *combien* (how much), etc.

TASK Q Tu reviens de tes vacances en France. Ecris une lettre à ton/ta correspondant(e) **en répondant à toutes ces questions en phrases complètes**.

(i)   Comment as-tu voyagé en France?

(ii) Comment était le voyage?

(iii) Où as-tu logé?

(iv) Qu'est-ce que tu as fait en France? Donne **deux** détails.

(v)   Quel temps faisait-il?

(vi) Qu'est-ce que tu penses de la France?

(vii) Tu iras où l'année prochaine?

WJEC 1998

Examiner's commentary Pay very careful attention to the different tenses required in answering these tasks. Tick off each task as you complete it.

Voici un article d'un magazine canadien.

Le Débat des Lecteurs

Camille (13 ans) nous a écrit: "Je travaille bien à l'école, parce que j'ai toujours rêvé de devenir professeur un jour. J'espère aussi voyager autour du monde. Je voudrais poser la question à vos lecteurs:

Comment voyez-vous votre avenir personnel?"

Donnez-nous des détails sur vos intentions pour l'avenir:
- la famille
- les études
- le travail
- les voyages
- vos rêves et vos ambitions

Écrivez un article pour répondre à la question de Camille.
Écrivez 120 mots environ.

SEG 1998

Examiner's commentary   Read the instructions carefully. You are writing about future ambitions here, so take care with your tenses.

There now follows a full sample Higher examination in speaking, reading and writing which gives you some extra material to practise prior to taking your exam for real in the summer.

After the exam papers, answers are given to the reading paper with some indication of how different marks would convert to different grades. However, you must remember that your final grade is based on your performance in all four skills. There are no 'correct answers' to the writing and speaking papers. The answers you give on these papers would have to be marked by an experienced teacher or examiner. So instead of answers, some notes are given.

The papers are of Higher Tier standard. They use different types of exercises that may be used by any Examination Board, but they may not correspond to the types that you will meet in the examination for which you are being prepared.

SPEAKING PAPER

You have *15 minutes* to prepare the three sections below.

1 Regardez cette image:

Vous téléphonez à un garage. Votre professeur joue le rôle de l'employé(e) au garage. Pendant la conversation, parlez de:
- ce qui s'est passé; • votre voiture; • où vous êtes; • qui est dans votre groupe.

2 Regardez ces dessins:

Racontez ces événements qui se sont passés la semaine dernière.

3 Parlez un peu de:
- ce que vous aimez faire pendant votre temps libre.
- comment vous avez passé les vacances de Noël.
- ce que vous espérez faire après avoir quitté l'école.

READING PAPER

Answer all the questions. Read the instructions and study the examples carefully. You may use a dictionary. Time allowed – *45 minutes*.

1 Lisez ce texte.

Mary Pierce était professionnelle de tennis à quatorze ans

Pour devenir une championne, Mary Pierce s'est entraînée depuis son enfance. Son père a été son premier entraîneur. Professionnelle à quatorze ans et demi, elle a remporté son premier tournoi à seize ans, en Sicile.

À vingt ans, Mary Pierce a déjà passé la moitié de sa vie à s'entraîner sur les courts de tennis. Jim Pierce, son père, lui a mis une raquette entre les mains dès l'âge de dix ans. Il lui donne un seul conseil: taper dans la balle le plus fort possible. À cette époque, Mary ne pensait pas devenir la championne qu'elle est aujourd'hui. «*Je ne faisais que jouer avec mes amis après l'école*», a-t-elle raconté après sa victoire en finale des Internationaux d'Australie.

Mary terrorisée

Son père veut en faire une championne. Il la pousse à s'entraîner. Il vend même sa maison et sa bijouterie pour se consacrer à l'entraînement de sa fille. À quatorze ans et demi, Mary devient joueuse professionnelle. Elle remporte son premier tournoi à Palerme, en Sicile, en 1991. Elle a alors seize ans. Mais Mary est terrorisée par le tyran qu'est son père. En 1993, elle se sépare de son père comme entraîneur. C'est le coach d'Agassi, Nick Bollettieri, qui le remplace. Suivi plus tard de Sven Groeneveld, l'entraîneur néerlandais d'Arantxa Sanchez. Grâce à eux, elle deviendra la championne que l'on connaît: «*Le rude travail a payé*», avoue aujourd'hui Mary.   **Olivier Gasselin**

Remplissez les blancs dans le texte suivant. Utilisez UN mot chaque fois, choisi dans la liste en-dessous.

Exemple: Mary Pierce est devenue *professionnelle* à l'âge de quatorze ans.

Elle a gagné un tournoi pour la première fois à l'âge de (1) .... ans. C'est

son (2) .... qui lui a acheté sa première raquette. Quand elle était jeune,

elle jouait au tennis pour le (3) .... Pour (4) .... son

entraînement, le père de Mary a vendu sa maison.

A partir de 1993 elle a le (5) .... coach qu'Agassi.

Choisissez les mots dans cette liste:
champion; consacrer; payer; vingt; ~~professionnelle~~; entraîner; seize; amis; comme; plaisir; remplace; père; remporter; même; quatorze; conseil.

QUESTIONS Des jeunes parlent de leur passe-temps.

Lisez ces extraits.

> **1** Je joue depuis cinq ou six ans maintenant. Je trouve que ça me détend. Je joue beaucoup de styles mais j'aime surtout le style classique. J'aime aussi accompagner les chanteurs.

> **2** J'ai visité presque tous les pays de l'Europe et j'aime en particulier l'Italie à cause de l'architecture. Je suis allée aussi en Afrique — en Tunisie. Mon rêve, c'est d'aller en Chine parce que c'est un pays qui me fascine.

> **3** Je fais des centaines de kilomètres par semaine. C'est une question d'entraînement — faut bien se tenir en forme parce que, en été, il y a de longues courses et des concours. J'ai déjà gagné deux médailles et une coupe. Des fois on a des problèmes comme des crevaisons, mais ce n'est pas grave.

> **4** Pour m'inspirer je sors, quel que soit le temps qu'il fait, je me promène et je réfléchis. Après quelque temps une idée me vient à l'esprit et je la développe. Je rentre chez moi et je l'écris et je travaille là-dessus jusqu'à ce que j'en sois satisfait. Ce n'est pas nécessaire que ça rime — l'important, c'est que ça vient du coeur.

> **5** Je me lève très tôt. J'y vais à bicyclette. Le voyage, je ne l'aime pas beaucoup mais tant pis. Une fois arrivée là, à la campagne, je me cache et j'attends. Il faut être très patient, et ne pas bouger. Je reste là et j'en vois de toutes les espèces. Des fois je prends mon magnétophone à piles avec moi pour enregistrer leurs chants. C'est si beau!

Exemple:
Je joue pour mon école et pour la ville, dans l'équipe des jeunes. Je joue avant-centre donc des fois je marque des buts — assez souvent, quoi! C'est un sport que j'adore.

Pour chaque personne choisissez dans cette liste le passe-temps qui correspond le mieux.

(a) écrire de la poésie.   (b) regarder les oiseaux.

(c) jouer du piano.   (d) faire du chant.

(e) faire du vélo.   (f) étudier des livres d'architecture.

(g) ~~jouer au football.~~   (h) étudier la campagne.

(i) voyager à l'étranger.   (j) faire des promenades.

Exemple: *g*

1 .... **2** .... **3** .... **4** .... **5** ......

3 Lisez ce texte.

JEAN-LOUIS ETIENNE

Jean-Louis Etienne, le premier-homme à avoir atteint le Pôle Nord à pied prépare une nouvelle expédition au Pôle Sud.

Jean-Louis Etienne, ses amis l'appellent le "savanturier"... comme savant et aventurier. Savant, parce qu'il est médecin. Aventurier, car il a été, tour à tour, marin dans la course autour du monde avec Tabarly, médecin dans le Paris-Dakar, et alpiniste sur l'Everest.

Puis, en 1986, Jean-Louis Etienne a accompli une "première", qui l'a fait connaître du public: il a marché pendant deux mois jusqu'au Pôle Nord, seul avec ses skis et un traîneau!

Six mois pour traverser le Pôle Sud

Aujourd'hui, il prépare une nouvelle aventure: six mois à travers l'Antarctique, le continent le plus hostile de la planète. Il compte partir d'août 1998 à février 1999. L'Antarctique, c'est aussi grand que l'Inde et la Chine réunies. Jusqu'ici, il n'a été traversé que deux fois, en avion et en voiture. Pour parcourir ces 7500 kilomètres de désert glacé, Jean-Louis Etienne, lui, utilisera des chiens de traîneau.

Jean-Louis Etienne veut partir avec cinq compagnons. Les deux piliers de l'expédition? L'Américain Will Steger, qui élève quatre-vingts chiens polaires, les plus résistants possible, en vue de l'expédition. Le Soviétique Viktor Boyarsky, spécialiste des questions d'environnement, est déjà allé quatre fois en Antarctique. Les trois autres – un Japonais, un Canadien et un Anglais – devront d'abord faire leurs preuves au cours d'un voyage d'entraînement au Groënland, en mai prochain.

Une température de –89°C !

L'Antarctique est l'un des endroits les plus froids` du globe. Le thermomètre y est déjà descendu à –89°C, au mois de juillet!

Comment vivre avec le froid extrême? Voici le conseil de Jean-Louis Etienne: "Pour mieux le supporter, il faut l'accepter. Cela vous évite de gaspiller de l'énergie à vouloir lutter contre lui."

Le froid ne sera pas l'obstacle majeur: "les crevasses seront notre plus gros problème. Elles peuvent être immenses et infranchissables avec les chiens et les traîneaux. Il faudra les contourner... sans perdre son chemin !"

© Okapi

Répondez à ces questions **en français**.

Exemple: Où Jean-Louis veut-il aller pour sa nouvelle expédition?

Au Pôle Sud

1 Expliquez le mot "savanturier".

.... (1)

2 Que fait Jean-Louis comme métier, en tant que "savant"?

.... (1)

3 En quelle année Jean-Louis est-il allé au Pôle Nord?

.... (1)

4 Il a mis combien de temps pour y arriver?

.... (1)

5 Avec qui est-il allé au Pôle Nord?

.... (1)

6 Quelle distance fera-t-il pour traverser le Pôle Sud?

.... (1)

7 De quel moyen de transport se servira-t-il?

.... (1)

8 Qui l'accompagnera pendant son voyage au Pôle Sud?

.... (1)

9 Quel temps fait-il au Pôle Sud?

.... (1)

10 Quel sera le plus grand danger pendant le voyage, selon Jean-Louis?

.... (1)

WRITING PAPER

You have *1 hour* to answer the following two questions.

1 Lisez cette lettre.

Avignon le 17 mai 1998

Salut !

C'est moi – ta correspondante française – Martine ! Ça va bien, j'espère. Tu as beaucoup de travail à faire à l'école en ce moment? Que penses-tu de l'école, toi ?

Pendant les vacances de Pâques, je suis allée voir ma famille en Bretagne. C'était formidable ! J'ai rencontré des jeunes de mon âge et on s'est bien marrés ensemble. Qu'est-ce que tu as fait pendant les vacances de Pâques, toi ?

Je t'écris pour te demander si tu voudrais venir chez moi cet été. Maman m'a dit que tu peux venir passer une semaine ou deux chez nous. Qu'est-ce que tu en penses ! Ça serait chouette, non ?

Écris-moi vite pour me dire si tu peux venir, quand et comment.

À bientôt de te lire.

Grosses bises

Martine.

Ecrivez une réponse à Martine. Ecrivez 100 à 120 mots **en français**. Répondez aux questions de Martine au sujet de:

- l'école;

- les vacances de Pâques;

- l'invitation pour l'été.

2   Regardez cette image.

Vous avez été témoin de cet accident. Ecrivez un rapport pour la police pour expliquer les circonstances de l'accident. Donnez votre opinion de la cause de l'accident.

Ecrivez environ 150 mots **en français**.

Answers

This section provides answers for the Listening and Reading exercises in this book.

LISTENING ANSWERS

Task		Answer	Mark
A	1	D	1
	2	B	1
	3	B	1
	4	A	1
	5	B	1

Examiner's tip You won't have had much trouble with these, but remember to learn thoroughly simple basics such as numbers, times, directions and so on. They will certainly come up in the exam. Don't assume that a certain letter will not be used more than another. Just because B has been used twice in the first four answers does not mean that it can't be used for the fifth. On Q.3, be careful to listen closely to the whole sentence. Candidates often hear part of the phrase (*sept heures*) and choose the answer immediately, without hearing that *et quart* follows.

Task		Answer	Mark
B	1	B	1
	2	F	1
	3	A	1
	4	C	1
	5	C	1
	6	E	1
	7	B	1

Examiner's tip Take your time to study the pictures and to be clear in your mind what each one represents. Note that in Q. 4–7 more than one drink or snack is mentioned, hence the need to listen carefully to the whole of each playing to establish which ones the customers finally choose. Note the very common use of the phrase *je prends* for 'I'll have'.

Task		Answer	Mark
C	1	A (head)	1
	2	C (four persons)	1
	3	Arrow pointing to 3rd floor	1
	4	B (chicken and chips)	1
	5	12:00	1
	6	A (table tennis)	1

Task		Answer	Mark
D	**1**	A	1
	2	B	1
	3	C	1

Examiner's tip You needn't worry too much if you don't fully understand the written and recorded introductions to each, as the choice of pictures makes it clear what the subject matter of each is. You do, however, need to listen carefully before choosing your answers. You will hear the other alternatives mentioned but they may not be appropriate; in Q.2, for example, other people are mowing the lawn or tidying the room and in Q.3 there is a disagreement about what to do next weekend.

Task			Answer	Mark
E	**1**		1 juillet au 28 septembre	1
	2		des lunettes (spéciales)	1
	3		Festival de Chant	1
	4	(i)	Québec (ii) Sénégal	1
	5		gratuit/rien	1
	6	(i)	à pied (ii) à patins à roulettes	1
	7		bassin tactile (pour toucher les poissons)	1
	8		21-30-98-98	1

Examiner's tip Make sure you know the word *gratuit*, used in Q.5; it often occurs in Listening and Reading exams.

Task		Answer	Mark
F		**PAUL**	
		professeur	1
		aime les enfants	1
		longues études (à l'université)	1
		AMÉLIE	
		garagiste	1
		aime les voitures	1
		fatigant/mal payé	1
		MARC	
		journaliste	1
		aime visiter les autres pays	1
		chômage	1

Examiner's tip As well as employment, the subject of unemployment is often mentioned. Be sure to learn *chômage* and *chômeur*.

Task	Answer	Mark
G	40 fr in 2nd error box	1
	pas d'alcool in 3rd error box	1
	mercredi in 5th error box	1

Examiner's tip Note that the details don't come in order. Note also that the mark total tells you how many errors there are likely to be.

Task		Answer	Mark
H	1	D	1
	2	H	1
	3	G	1
	4	A	1
	5	C	1
	6	B	1

Examiner's tip In exercises of this type, don't expect to hear the particular keyword such as *circulation, crime, sport*, etc. You are being tested on your ability to understand the general 'gist' of the extract, therefore you mustn't worry if you don't understand each word. Be careful of the pitfalls, however. The sports extract (Q.2) starts by mentioning the weather (so does the road report in Q.5), but this is not the main subject matter of the extract.

Task	Answer	Mark
I	True statements: (b); (c); (d); (f); (h); (j); (k).	7

Examiner's tip Don't pick the true statements until you have heard the conversation twice. This is a tricky exercise which requires careful listening. Don't expect to hear the words in the statements on the recording – gist understanding involves matching *Il a plu sans arrêt* to the words in (b) or *La prochaine fois tu pourrais venir avec nous* to statement (f). At the same time, beware of the easily-made mistakes – phrase (g), for example, is wrong simply because of the word *voir*.

Task		Answer	Mark
J	1	Alain.	1
	2	Mme Duval and Marie.	2
	3	Alain.	1
	4	Mme Duval	1
	5	Mme Duval – n'a pas une opinion très forte.	1
		Alain – est plutôt contre le Tunnel.	1
		Marie – est plutôt pour le Tunnel.	1

Task	Answer	Mark

Examiner's tip Did you notice that five marks are available for the first four questions and that therefore two boxes had to be ticked for one of the opinions? Be sure to read the statements carefully before hearing the conversation.

Task	Answer	Mark
K 1	7h15 à 7h30	1
2	il a oublié sa valise/ses bagages	1
3	des embouteillages/beaucoup de circulation	1
4	tombe en panne d'essence	1
5	B	1
6	il a plu/il pleut; il a grêlé/(il) grêle	2
7	il a raté la sortie; il n'a pas quitté l'autoroute	1
8	D	1
9	A	1

Examiner's tip Note that in answering questions in French, it is your understanding of French, not your ability to write it that is being tested. It is perfectly OK to use figures in Q.1, but the time range must be shown. Sentences are not required. There are alternatives to the above answers; on Q.2, for example, *pour sa valise* is quite acceptable.

Task	Answer	Mark
L (a)	Needs to be in Calais by midday; otherwise he might miss the ferry; English friends are waiting for him at Dover; he can't contact them.	3
(b)	Farmers.	1
(c)	They should take their case to the government rather than troubling the holiday makers.	3

Examiner's tip (a) With three marks available, write down all that you understand, but don't guess if you are not sure of the meaning. Don't forget the verb *manquer*, 'to miss', and remember that the French call Dover *Douvres* (as they call London *Londres*). (c) Although there are again three marks available, there are not three separate details. Here you draw your conclusion about why the traffic is at a standstill; the point is that the farmers are making a protest by blocking the road.

READING ANSWERS

Task	Answer	Mark
A	Un gâteau = Boulangerie/Pâtisserie	1
	Des timbres = Tabac	1
	Des bananes = Marchand de fruits et légumes	1
	Du pain = Boulangerie/Pâtisserie	1
	Du shampooing = Pharmacie	1
	Des saucisses = Charcuterie	1

Task	Answer	Mark

Always study the example carefully. It is designed to show you how to proceed. This means that if you are not fully confident about the meaning of the French instructions, the example should make things quite clear. Notice that there are more products than shops but that you must indicate where each product is bought.

B	**1**	A (12 F 50)	1
	2	A	1
	3	C	1

Q.2 The phrase *défense de* should be learned. It is used with a verb to mean 'is not allowed'.

C	**(i)**	B	1
	(ii)	F	1
	(iii)	A	1
	(iv)	C	1
	(v)	D	1

Don't forget that *bibliothèque* means 'library' but that *librairie* means 'bookshop'. Another favourite with exam setters!

D	**1**	D (21.00)	1
	2	D (page 14)	1

Here, the skill tested is that of scanning material in order to pinpoint the answer. Note that in the second example, only four pages are mentioned in the choice of answers so clearly you only need to concentrate on those. Learn the word *météorologie* (often shortened to *météo*) for 'weather forecast'.

E	**(a)**	A	1
	(b)	E	1
	(c)	C	1

Learn the phrases denoting prohibition – *défense de...*, *il est défendu de...* and *(il est) interdit de...*

F	**1**	C (Gratin de légumes)	1

Task		Answer		Mark
2		A (Boissons)		1

Task		Answer		Mark
G		8h30 Français		1
		9h30 Anglais		1
		10h30 Sciences		1
		11h30 Maths		1
		2h00 Maths		1
		3h00 Dessin		1
		4h00 Dessin		1
H		Faible:	Education Physique et sportive	1
		Travailleur:	Mathématiques	1
		Insolent:	Anglais	1
		Paresseux:	Français	1
		Bavard:	Histoire-Géographie	1
		Timide:	Dessin	1

Task		Answer	Mark
I	1	(elle a) deux (frères)	1
	2	(c'est) très bien (fait)	1
	3	elle aime manger les choses sucrées/elle s'inquiète à propos de sa santé	1
	4	pour voir ses copains (et ses copines)	1
	5	au bord de la mer	1
	6	Céline accueillira sa correspondante/la correspondante de Céline viendra avec l'échange	1

Task	Answer	Mark
J	The missing words should be in this order, with one mark for each one: *été*; *bruns*; *parlé*; *s'appelle*; *téléphone*.	5

Task		Answer	Mark
K	**(a)**	chirurgien	**1**
	(b)	Allemagne	**1**
	(c)	(i) il s'occupe de moutons	**1**

> **Examiner's tip** Once again notice how brief answers are perfectly acceptable.

L	**(i)**	18 ans	**1**
	(ii)	entraînement	**1**
	(iii)	jeans (1); baskets (1)	**2**
	(iv)	3 ans	**1**
	(v)	méchante	**1**
	(vi)	est allée au club de plus en plus OR elle est entrée dans une école de glace OR elle ne voulait pas quitter la piste	**2**
	(vii)	(elle est) professionnelle maintenant	**1**

> **Examiner's tip** Always be on the look-out for questions carrying two marks; either two points will be required (as in Q.(iii)) or a more complex answer will be expected (as in Q.(vi)).

M	**1**	FAUX	**1**
	2	VRAI	**1**
	3	VRAI	**1**
	4	FAUX	**1**
	5	VRAI	**1**
	6	FAUX	**1**

> **Examiner's tip** Once you have read and understood the questions, some of them can be answered through common sense (although of course you must always refer to the text as well). There is some useful travel vocabulary in this passage which you should learn.

N	**1**	VRAI	**1**
	2	FAUX	**1**
		L'été des collégiens	**1**
	3	FAUX	**1**
		C'est pour les jeunes qui ne vont pas en vacances OR C'est pour les jeunes qui restent dans le département.	**1**
	4	FAUX	**1**
		C'est aussi d'apprendre la nature/la lecture d'une carte/la botanique, etc. (any example given of a non-sporting activity)	**1**

Task	Answer	Mark
5	VRAI	1
6	FAUX	1
	Elle se répétera/continuera, etc.	1

Examiner's tip As with any Higher Tier exercise, read text and questions very carefully and check your answers. Don't look up every word in your dictionary (you won't have time). Look up key words in the questions such as *supprimer* (Q.5). Don't forget, incidentally, that the verbs you look for in the dictionary are given in the INFINITIVE only – so you wouldn't find *supprimée*, for instance.

O	**(a)**	Jean-Jacques	1
	(b)	Carole	1
	(c)	Karine	1
	(d)	Carole	1
	(e)	Jean-Jacques	1
	(f)	Jean-Jacques	1
	(g)	Carole	1
	(h)	Karine	1

Examiner's tip Look for words in the statements which match words in the texts – e.g. *climat/neige*; *nourriture/repas*; *devait se lever/on m'a réveillé*, etc.

P	**1**	H	1
	2	M	1
	3	S	1
	4	P	1
	5	N	1
	6	H	1

Examiner's tip This is not an easy exercise. All extracts need to be read carefully several times before making your choice. As in the last exercise, look for key words in the statements which match similar words in the extracts – e.g. *espaces* (Q.6) and *endroits* (H); *une activité dangereuse* (Q.3) and *de graves accidents* (P). Note and learn the phrases used here for expressing opinion (and use them in Speaking and Writing) – *je pense que...; je crois que...; je trouve que...; à mon avis*.

Q		Any four of the following five points:
	(i)	the bridegroom's brother fell ill during the wedding (suffering from sunstroke)

Reading answers

Task	Answer	Mark
(ii)	the bride had an asthma attack	
(iii)	the car taking the couple to the airport caught fire	
(iv)	the couple's house was burgled	
(v)	the video-recording of the wedding was stolen	1 mark each, max 4 **4**

Examiner's tip In order to refer to the correct people, take note of the genders of *le (du) marié* (masculine) – 'the bridegroom' and *la mariée* (feminine) – 'the bride'.

R (a)	every day	1
(b)	50 francs	1
(c)	no	1
(d)	it's filtered all the time	1
(e)	you can buy sandwiches there or bring your own food	1
(f)	have a rest in special areas	1

Examiner's tip Don't confuse *repas* (meal/s) with *repos* (rest).

S (a)	he got 400,000 votes in the Japanese Senate elections	1
(b)	he realised his records were selling there	1
(c)	he loved the country; he fell in love with Yoshiko; he married her (any two)	1
(d)	Yoshiko didn't enjoy living in France	1
(e)	he realises that there are still people dying of hunger and cold	1
(f)	he still loves it but doesn't feel it's home any more	1

T 1	so that they can be recognised	1
2	if he/she arrives 5 minutes late; if an expected letter doesn't arrive	2
3	because of the hours they work, they cannot go out late with friends	1
4	B	1

Examiner's tip You need to read this long passage carefully before attempting the questions. Use the dictionary wisely – don't look up each word that you don't know. Make brief notes about the general meaning of each paragraph and then try the questions.

84